Love
yn ♡♡
mine +

MARTYN LAWRENCE BULLARD
FABRIC

Darya ikat
174834 Jewel
Martyn Lawrence Bullard F11

LIVE
LOVE
& DECORATE
Martyn Lawrence Bullard

LIVE

LOVE

& DECORATE

Martyn Lawrence Bullard

PHOTOGRAPHY BY TIM STREET-PORTER

I would like to dedicate this book to my late father,
Leonard Bullard, who always
believed in me 100 percent, whatever I did.

First published in the United States of America in 2011
by Rizzoli International Publications, Inc.
300 Park Avenue South
New York, NY 10010
www.rizzoliusa.com

© 2011 by Martyn Lawrence Bullard
Foreword © Sir Elton John
All photographs are © Tim Street-Porter except for the following:
Douglas Friedman, p. 222
Harry Benson, p. 28
Firooz Zahedi, p. 166
John Ellis, pp. 70–71
François Dischinger, pp. 141,148
Deborah Anderson, p. 63

2011 2012 2013 / 10 9 8 7 6 5 4 3 2 1

Printed in China

Design by Doug Turshen with David Huang

ISBN: 978-0-8478-3676-5

Library of Congress Control Number: 2011924689

TABLE OF CONTENTS

FOREWORD BY SIR ELTON JOHN

I love my homes almost as much as I love performing onstage, and I have worked with many decorators over the years to create these special spaces. My homes have always been my sanctuary, my castle, my private paradise, and as such, they have reflected my evolving taste and been my experiment and discovery ground. My home is a way to express myself and to display my collections (of which there are many). Each of my homes has a different vibe, a different angle of my personality, and a different interpretation of my life and that of my partner, David.

So when we decided to create a new home in L.A., we turned immediately to Martyn—not only a talented designer but our close friend. This friendship, and his understanding of our lives, likes, dislikes, and idiosyncrasies, made him the perfect choice. The project flowed so easily. Our mutual love of beauty, luxury, fantasy, drama, casual entertaining, comfort, and all things decorative led to the creation of a perfect home nestled high above the bustling L.A. streets. Martyn worked hand in hand with David, and together they made my floating jewel box into a reality.

Now, not only do we love our L.A. home, it has also become the hub of family life with our son, Zachary, the perfect addition to our lives. Of all the beautiful art and treasures that surround me, none is more precious than him. And the spectacular apartment that Martyn designed for us is the perfect setting to bring our adored son home to. As Martyn says, we live, we love, and he decorates!

—*Elton John*

A DETAIL OF ELTON AND DAVID'S LIVING ROOM WITH THE POWERFUL WANG GUANGYI PAINTING TAKING CENTER STAGE. THE CUSTOM-MADE SOFA IS COVERED IN A NUBBY SILK TWEED FROM B & B ITALIA FABRICS. THE SKULL SCULPTURE ON THE COFFEE TABLE WAS CARVED FROM A SOLID PIECE OF ROCK CRYSTAL, AND THE GLASS SPUTNIK IS VINTAGE VENINI.

INTRODUCTION

Interior design is my life. I live it and breathe it and wake up feeling lucky to be doing something I love. But the story of how I got here is amazing. I call it my Hollywood tale in reverse.

My earliest memories are as a young boy playing with my sister's dollhouse. I would rearrange the furniture, mold bits of silver foil into chandeliers, create art with postage stamps, and use cassette tape boxes to build rooms. My mother says I used to draw houses on a chalkboard and add stick furniture to the inside of the rooms. I realize now that this must have been the decorator gene rearing its head.

I never realized that being an interior designer was even a possibility. Instead I unknowingly taught myself the trade and learned the knowledge of periods, decorative styles, age, and design by buying and selling small antique items. As a twelve-year-old boy I started to buy and sell things: dishes, silver spoons, boxes, pieces of fabric—anything I thought was pretty and I could make a profit on. My father took me early on Saturday mornings to rent a stall at the Greenwich Antiques Market in South London, and I ran around to all the other vendors buying what I thought was interesting or beautiful with my pocket money. Then I would bring things back to my stall, display them on draped cloths and raised boxes, and make them look as appealing as possible to the bemused public, who would wander by and purchase these pieces from this precocious teenager with a sparkle in his eye and a great story to go along with his wares. I learned what was popular from my mistakes and my successes. My stock grew, as did my knowledge of the items I was buying and selling.

By the age of sixteen I had a marvelous following of dealers and collectors who would flock around my stool to see what I had to sell that day. I would sell to the best dealers in London, like Genevieve from the legendary Guinevere

A PETER BEARD PHOTOGRAPH IS BALANCED BY A SEVENTEENTH-CENTURY BLOOD-RED CHEST IN THE ENTRY OF ALLENE LAPIDES'S SANTA FE RANCH.

Antiques Shop on the King's Road, to Toby, the head buyer for the Ralph Lauren antiques and accessories department, who shipped the pieces to the U.S. to dress the windows of Madison Avenue and Rodeo Drive.

With my profits I started my own collection of wondrous things: Georgian tea caddies, small boxes of ivory, silver and stone inlay, old iron stone decorative plates, transfer-ware china, and anything beautiful that I just couldn't part with. I decorated my bedroom with red and gold damask fabrics swagged onto a four-poster bed inspired by my visit to Napoleon's empress Josephine's Malmaison, which had wowed me with all its Empire glamour. I still have some of these treasures, which have traveled all over the world with me.

By the time I was seventeen, I started to dream of acting, my father's original career. I continued to buy and sell antiques, which now included silver items and gold jewelry, but now with the goal of making money to put myself through drama school. By the time I left college I had saved enough money through my antique dealing and a few modeling jobs and fashion shows to take a course at the Lee Strasberg Actors Studio in Covent Garden, London. I took the course for nine months, learning plays, performing scenes, doing sense memory exercises, and generally having great fun—so much fun, in fact, that I decided I wanted to become a Hollywood star. The first step was enrolling in the Strasberg Institute in Los Angeles. I went back to working all the best London antiques markets for three months, buying and selling frantically to raise money for my L.A. adventure.

Once I had made a couple thousand dollars, I paid my tuition in advance and bought myself a ticket to my dreams. But upon arriving in L.A. and starting my classes, I found my dreams might take a little longer than I thought. I took my classes, acted out my scenes, and auditioned for agents, but nothing happened. I was now broke, so I worked part-time in a coffee shop, thinking that was another way to get discovered, until finally I fell back on my trained eye and started to search the L.A. flea markets for treasures. I bought a diamond-studded tiepin from a box of junk at the Rose Bowl for $5, which I turned around and sold for $500. Suddenly I was off again with my newfound capital. I bought and sold small decorative items and jewelry, using my talent for display to lure in the customers. Quickly I gained a following and started making money to keep me in drama school.

Finally the ice broke. I started to get the odd part here, an extra part there, and even landed a few little roles. I was cast to play Eartha Kitt's boy-toy pianist in Ed Woods's last movie, *I Woke Up Early the Day I Died*. Little did I know this fleeting role would lead me to my real vocation.

By chance I befriended the producer and one day invited him and his girlfriend over to the tiny but charming house I was renting in West Hollywood. They loved it. All my flea market treasures and collections were mixed with beaten-up antique furniture I had bought at the swap meets and weekend antiques shows. By the end of dinner the producer asked me to come help decorate their new offices, The Hollywood Film Works. I was excited, not so much by the opportunity to decorate, but I thought if I did a good job I would get cast in another movie. I set to work scouring the local flea markets for French leather club chairs. I hung old wooden Indian doors on the walls as art, bought wood-bladed fans for the high-beamed ceilings to create motion and add a colonial air, and sunk grass cloth into the cabinet doors for texture. It was sort of British Raj meets Raffles, with a touch of Casablanca drama. The look was a great success—all done on a shoestring budget, a wish, and a prayer.

The day it was finished I received a call from Liz Heller, who was then the V.P. at Capital Records. She loved the Film Works offices she had just visited, and could I come look at her office and new home? I was flabbergasted. Not having had any training, and literally flying by the seat of my pants, I went and met Liz. It was best friends at first sight, and I immediately started decorating for her and her fiancé, John Manulis.

We had been merrily working on their projects when disaster struck with their wedding planner. I had to jump in and help out. With staple gun in hand, flowers from the mart, and fabrics from the local dress-making store, I whipped up a Moroccan-themed look and got myself invited to the festivities. I was seated that evening next to Cheryl Tiegs, an American icon and the world's first supermodel. By the end of the evening Cheryl had asked me to look at her new house: a 1950s bungalow in Bel Air that desperately needed reinventing. Together we set about this task, I took a partner, got a green card, and opened Martynus, a bona fide interior design office in West Hollywood. By the time Cheryl's house was finished, a buzz had already started. Soon our newly created Balinese colonial pavilion appeared in *Elle Décor* and graced the covers of magazines around the world. Presto! A design career was born, and I've never looked back.

So my Hollywood dream has come true—not the one I thought, but the one fate laid out for me. The moral to this decorator's tale is to always follow your dreams, even if you're not quite sure where they will take you. And always live, love, and decorate.

A Model Life

SUPERMODEL CHERYL TIEGS
AT HOME IN BEL AIR

This house holds a very special place in my heart. It was the first real design job I ever did. I learned so much from it and forged a lifelong friendship with its owner, Cheryl Tiegs.

We met at the wedding of mutual friends of ours, Liz Heller and John Manulis. I had helped Liz pull the wedding together, and she sat me next to Cheryl. A few days later Cheryl called and asked me to come look at her new home, a Polynesian tiki-style 1950s teardown on one of the best streets in Bel Air. We sat on the floor together looking at this dated bungalow, and I listened as Cheryl described her dream to make it into a Balinese pavilion. Neither of us had been to Bali at that point and really didn't know what that meant. Even more incredible was that I had no portfolio to show her. Cheryl had interviewed the top designers from both coasts to do her home, yet amazingly she went with her hunch and chose me. It was overwhelming, exciting, scary, and a dream come true, all at once.

Over the years we have continued to work together on this house, through many changes in our lives. The home has been witness to weddings, divorces, charity events, TV shoots, countless parties (including my fortieth birthday party, which Cheryl hosted for me), and, most important, to our enduring friendship. It is a labor of love that has stood the test of time. Like a fine wine, it seems to keep getting better with age.

OPPOSITE: AN EIGHTEENTH-CENTURY TANSU CABINET HOUSES CHERYL'S ARCHIVE OF HUNDREDS OF MAGAZINES BEARING HER IMAGE ON THEIR COVERS. THE FRUITWOOD LOUIS XV FAUTEUIL IS UPHOLSTERED IN A GOLDEN BLOND ZEBRA HIDE. **PREVIOUS PAGES, LEFT:** ABOVE THE STONE FIREPLACE IN CHERYL'S BEDROOM, PREVIOUSLY A WINDOW SURROUND FROM THE DEMOLISHED BANK OF NEW YORK, IS HER PORTRAIT BY ANDY WARHOL. **RIGHT:** ASSORTED SUZANI AND IKAT PILLOWS DECORATE A SAPPHIRE BLUE MANUEL CANOVAS VELVET SOFA. THE LAMPS ON THE CHINESE TABLE BEHIND WERE ONCE FINIALS ON THE TOP OF AN ANCIENT INDONESIAN BUILDING. THE RED LACQUERED HATBOX BETWEEN THEM IS EIGHTEENTH CENTURY.

"This creation, my magical Balinese paradise, helps soothe my soul in this hectic world." —CHERYL TIEGS

ABOVE: SITTING IN FRONT OF A PRECIOUS SEVENTEENTH-CENTURY SCREEN FROM THE CHINESE PORCELAIN COMPANY IN NEW YORK IS A COLLECTION OF NINETEENTH-CENTURY GREEN WARE AND A GLASS BOTTLE SALVAGED FROM A SHIPWRECKED SPANISH GALLEON. THE BRASS CANDLESTICK IS DUTCH. **OPPOSITE:** THE GREAT-ROOM COLUMNS WERE HAND PAINTED BY RICHARD PETITE USING TRADITIONAL INDONESIAN MOTIFS. EDWARDIAN-STYLE CLUB CHAIRS ARE UPHOLSTERED IN SUZANI BY DONGHIA. **FOLLOWING PAGES:** THE LIVING ROOM MARBLE FIREPLACE WAS ONCE A PORTAL TO AN INDIAN TEMPLE. THE COFFEE TABLE IS FROM ROSE TARLOW.

OPPOSITE: THE NINETEENTH-CENTURY DINING TABLE ONCE SERVED AS A PICNIC TABLE FOR THE GOVERNOR'S MANSION IN JAVA. IT IS LAID WITH ANTIQUE WEDGEWOOD "CABBAGE" WARE AND WILLIAM YEOWARD CRYSTAL. TOP LEFT: CHERYL AND ME IN HER GARDEN. TOP RIGHT: A PINK IKAT PILLOW FROM NATHAN TURNER BRINGS LIFE TO THE SOFA. CENTER LEFT: A CARVED TEAK PANEL SERVES AS A ROOM DIVIDER. THE COPPER PLANTER WAS ORIGINALLY BURIED IN THE GROUND AND USED TO DYE BATIK FABRICS. THE POLYCHROMED INDIAN CHAIR DATES FROM 1850. CENTER: A REVERSE-PAINTED GLASS CHINESE ANCESTOR PAINTING SITS ON A REGENCY TABLE TOP INLAID WITH A ROMAN MOSAIC EXCAVATED FROM POMPEII. CENTER RIGHT: AN ANTIQUE CARVED WOOD STAG HEAD IS MOUNTED TO THE TEAK WALL PANELS. LEFT: NINETEENTH-CENTURY INDIAN COLORED GLASS HUNDI LANTERNS FOUND ON LONDON'S PORTOBELLO ROAD ILLUMINATE THE DINING ROOM.

ABOVE: AN INDO-DUTCH COLONIAL CHANDELIER DATING FROM THE LATE NINETEENTH CENTURY HANGS ABOVE THE KITCHEN ISLAND. THE WALLS WERE STENCILED BY MICHAEL FOULKROD USING INDONESIAN MOTIFS. THE TIN CEILING WAS PAINTED EGG BLUE FROM FARROW AND BALL, AND THE WATERWORKS FARMHOUSE SINK AND FIXTURES COMPLETE THE VINTAGE FEELING. ECO-FRIENDLY CAMBRIA STONE WAS USED FOR THE FLOORS AND COUNTERTOPS. LEFT: CHERYL'S SON WAS VERY HANDS-ON IN THE REDESIGN OF HIS BEDROOM. HE HELPED THE ARTIST PAINT THE TATTOO ON THE CEILING. THE STARK ZEBRA CARPET TIES THE THEME TO THE REST OF THE HOUSE. OPPOSITE, TOP LEFT: AN EIGHTEENTH-CENTURY CHINESE CABINET DOUBLES AS TOWEL STORAGE AND DISPLAY FOR CHERYL'S PRECIOUS ANTIQUE AFRICAN BOOKS AND PERSONAL MEMENTOS. TOP RIGHT: IN THE DRESSING ROOM THE SINK WAS DESIGNED AS A PROFESSIONAL AREA, WITH LIGHT EVENLY FED TO THE SPACE FROM SIDE PANELS—IDEAL FOR APPLYING MAKEUP AND STYLING HAIR (SUPERMODEL REQUISITES). RIGHT: IN CHERYL'S BEDROOM A CUSTOM-MADE HALF-TESTER BED WAS EBONIZED TO ADD A COLONIAL VIBE. THE WALLS WERE STENCILED BY RICHARD PETITE FROM A CUSTOM ONE-OFF STENCIL WE MADE EXCLUSIVELY FOR THE ROOM. IT IS COMPOSED OF SEVEN LAYERS OF TEA STAIN AND COLOR PIGMENT. THE EMBROIDERED BEDDING IS BY DEBORAH SHARPE LINENS. PREVIOUS PAGES, LEFT: A NINETEENTH-CENTURY CARVED LAVA STONE BUDDHA HEAD FOUND AT PRIMARY SOURCE SITS ON THE HILLSIDE GUARDING THE POOL. RIGHT: A TEAK CHAIR, DRESSED IN MY BODRUM STRIPE PILLOW, WITH A COPPER RAIN DRUM THAT DOUBLES AS A SIDE TABLE.

High-Rise Haven

CHER'S HOLLYWOOD PENTHOUSE
PIED-À-TERRE

Cher has lived her life on a stage in one way or another since she was seventeen years old. So when she asked me to decorate her pied-à-terre in West Hollywood, I quickly realized that designing this amazing two-floor apartment was going to be no ordinary remodel. It needed to outshine any set she had ever set foot upon. Fantasy was the directive: an Indian fantasy to be exact. Cher wanted a home fit for a maharani or a Turkish princess. "I love all things exotic, Babe, Oriental, Zen, and magical," she said. Cher, known for her exuberant themed interiors over the years, was over her Gothic period and had become entranced with Buddhism and all the decorative trappings that such a meditative life encompasses.

The very first thing I bought for her was a nineteenth-century ivory painted tablet depicting an Indian deity. This small artwork inspired our palette of textured creams, tea-stained browns, ivory, chocolate, ebony, gold, bronze, and touches of rich merlot. Next a heavily carved triple-arch entryway reclaimed from a Rajasthan palace was used to ground the architecture and become the backdrop for her majestic bed, creating the instant magic Cher had desired.

The apartment that now contains items from India, Tibet, Turkey, Sri Lanka, China, Indonesia, Morocco, and Syria was revealed to her for the first time in its finished state during a surprise birthday party thrown by her close friends: me, jewelry designer Loree Rodkin, and designers Richard and Laurie Lynn Stark. Complete with spicy Indian fare, bare-chested turban-topped waiters, and three hundred candles of all sizes imaginable, the truly Orientalist soiree welcomed Hollywood's most exotic icon to her magical new home.

OPPOSITE: CHER IN HER WEST HOLLYWOOD HOME. PHOTOGRAPH BY HARRY BENSON. **PREVIOUS PAGES:** FROM THE LIVING ROOM, SLIDING DOORS DISAPPEAR TO REVEAL A VIEW OF LOS ANGELES AND THE OCEAN. THE TERRACE BECOMES PART OF THE LIVING ROOM WITH THE CAREFUL PLACEMENT OF FURNITURE, INCLUDING A CUSTOM-MADE INDIAN-STYLE CHAISE COVERED IN SUMMIT OUTDOOR FABRICS AND A SMALL TURKISH TABLE.

"I wanted something ethnic,
spicy, and romantic." —CHER

ABOVE: CHER'S APARTMENT IS ENTERED THROUGH BRONZE-STUDDED DOORS AND PAST BACKLIT, REVERSE-PAINTED GLASS PANELS DEPICTING INDIAN DEITIES BY KELLY HOLDEN. AN ANTIQUE INDIAN CARVED-WOOD PORTAL FRAMES THE ENTRANCE. THE GLASS LANTERN CAME FROM THE GRAND BAZAAR IN ISTANBUL. **OPPOSITE:** A DETAIL OF A SHAGREEN-TOPPED COFFEE TABLE WITH AN ANCIENT CHINESE GUAN YIN STATUE ON TOP OF AN INDIAN MARBLE-INLAID JAPATI TRAY. AN EARLY-TWENTIETH-CENTURY TIBETAN TAPESTRY IS WOVEN OF PURE GOLD THREAD AND SILVER PEYOTES.

TOP: MASHRABIYA SCREENS DISGUISE THE KITCHEN.
RIGHT: CHINESE TINKER'S LANTERNS LIGHT THE TERRACE.
OPPOSITE, TOP LEFT: INDONESIAN BRONZE GONGS
DECORATE THE STAIRWELL. TOP RIGHT: MASHRABIYA
SCREENS WERE ALSO USED IN THE POWDER ROOM.
BOTTOM: A CUSTOM-MADE L-SHAPE SOFA ALLOWS CHER
TO ENJOY HER CITY VIEWS. PREVIOUS PAGES: CHER'S
BEDROOM SITTING AREA HAS THREE CUSTOM-DESIGNED
SOFAS COVERED IN CORDED SILK. THE COFFEE TABLE WAS
INSPIRED BY DORIS DUKE'S DINING TABLE AT SHANGRI LA.

ABOVE: A DETAIL OF A NINETEENTH-CENTURY INDIAN TEMPLE CARVING GUARDS THE ENTRY TO CHER'S BEDROOM. **RIGHT:** A SIXTEENTH-CENTURY CHINESE MARRIAGE BED MADE OF ELM IS USED FOR GUESTS AND ALSO ACTS AS A PRIVATE TV NOOK FOR CHER (A TELEVISION IS INSTALLED INSIDE A HIDDEN PANEL). LARGE ANTIQUE INDIAN WATER VESSELS BALANCE THE SCALE OF THE BED, WHILE TURKISH LANTERNS WITH TEA-STAINED SILK SHADES GIVE SUBTLE ILLUMINATION. **PREVIOUS PAGES:** CHER'S DRAMATIC BED WAS MADE FROM ANTIQUE ARCHITECTURAL ELEMENTS SALVAGED FROM THE INDIAN ARCHES BEHIND THE BED THAT LEAD TO HER DRESSING ROOM. THE BED'S BOTTOM PANEL DROPS OPEN TO REVEAL A HYDRAULIC FLAT-SCREEN TV THAT RISES AT THE TOUCH OF A BUTTON. I BROUGHT THE HANGING LANTERNS BACK FROM MARRAKESH.

OPPOSITE, TOP: THE BATHTUB IS CLAD IN EIGHTEENTH-CENTURY CARVED PANELS FROM AN INDIAN PALACE. THE FOLDING HAREM CHAIRS ARE NINETEENTH-CENTURY SYRIAN. THE IVORY-INLAID ELEPHANT IS ONE OF CHER'S FAVORITE OBJECTS IN THE APARTMENT. FAR LEFT: THE INDIAN IVORY PAINTED TABLET WAS THE FIRST PURCHASE I MADE FOR THE APARTMENT AND HELPED DETERMINE OUR COLOR PALETTE. LEFT: INDIAN MERMAID GODDESS HANDLES ARE CAST IN BRONZE. ABOVE: THE EBONY ELEPHANT WAS MADE IN DELHI IN THE 1880S. I FOUND IT AT THE OLYMPIA FAIR FROM THE FAMOUS LONDON DEALER BLANCHARDS. TOP RIGHT: A DETAIL OF THE KELLY HOLDEN–PAINTED PANELS THAT ARE ILLUMINATED FROM BEHIND AND CAST A SEXY LIGHT IN THE ENTRY. RIGHT: HAND-EMBROIDERED SILK PILLOWS FROM ANICHINI DRESS CHER'S BED.

Villa Swanson

MY HOLLYWOOD HILLS
HIDEAWAY

I believe destiny plays a role in all aspects of life. I had visited Tim Street-Porter and Annie Kelly's magical Villa Vallombrosa many times, and I loved its charms and the old European style of Whitley Heights, where the house is situated. In September 2003 I was on a shoot for *Architectural Digest* with Tim in Santa Fe, and he mentioned that the house across the street was about to go on the market. That was on a Saturday. By Monday I had flown back to L.A., seen the house, fallen in love with it, and bought it. I have lived here in bliss ever since. The house has one of those rare qualities that make people automatically comfortable. The odd-shaped rooms, curved walls, well-worn floors, and uneven lath and plaster walls seem to transport you to a secret ancient villa in the Umbrian Hills or the old town of Seville.

The architecture is not just the star here; it's the history that provokes visitors to imagine all that has gone on here in its colorful past. Built in 1922, the house was first the home of Rudolph Valentino. Legend has it he placed the Portuguese plaque in the courtyard wall for good luck. Some of the sconces in the house are from his original decorative scheme.

Next, and giving the home its namesake, Gloria Swanson moved in, complete with maid and chauffeur. She created the dining room by enclosing the sun porch, and her French chandelier hangs there to this day, providing me with endless stories to dazzle my dinner guests with as we guess who also ate dinner under this fixture: Chaplin, Chevalier, Harlow, and Fairbanks Jr. (all once neighbors in this historic aerie).

OPPOSITE: AN ENGLISH SILVER-CLAD CORNUCOPIA IS FILLED WITH HYDRANGEAS. THE *SECRETAIRE* IS ITALIAN MILANESE WORK FROM THE EIGHTEENTH CENTURY. **PREVIOUS PAGES, LEFT:** A VIEW FROM THE INTERIOR COURTYARD OF THE BALCONY OFF MY BEDROOM, WHERE WILLIAM FAULKNER USED TO WRITE HIS SCREENPLAYS. **RIGHT:** A DETAIL OF A DENISE DE LA RUE PHOTOGRAPH OF A MEXICAN BULLFIGHTER AND A PILLOW MADE OF FABRIC FROM MY COLLECTION FOR SCHUMACHER.

After Swanson moved out in the 1950s, the house became the writing atelier of William Faulkner. He wrote some of his most famous screenplay adaptations while seated on the terrace off my bedroom. I still feel his creative spirit when I take in a little sun on that terrace during lazy weekend afternoons.

I have tried to keep up the traditions set forth by this illustrious list of previous homeowners. From parties for two hundred to intimate pizza and movie nights, I frequently entertain in my home, filling it with flickering candlelight. This special house has a life of its own, and I am intoxicated by the magic and creative energy that have soaked into its walls.

ABOVE: A VIEW OF THE FRONT OF MY HOUSE WITH ITS ORIGINAL IRONWORK DATING FROM 1923. OPPOSITE, TOP LEFT: THE MOTHER-OF-PEARL–INLAID TRAY IN MY LIVING ROOM WITH A ROMAN GLASS VESSEL, A CHINESE SILVER DISH, AND AN INDIAN SILVER TRIVET. TOP RIGHT: THE INNER COURTYARD WITH A PORTUGUESE PLAQUE PLACED IN THE GARDEN BY RUDOLPH VALENTINO. BOTTOM: THE GARDEN SOFAS ARE UPHOLSTERED IN ZANZIBAR FROM MY OUTDOOR FABRIC COLLECTION.

THE FAR END OF THE LIVING
ROOM ALSO SERVES AS
A CASUAL DINING AREA.
HIDDEN IN THE WALL IS
A LARGE TV SCREEN.
THE DENISE DE LA RUE
PHOTOGRAPHS OF FAMED
MEXICAN BULLFIGHTERS
WERE PURCHASED AT
THE GAGOSIAN GALLERY
IN L.A. THE ZEBRA RUG
ONCE BELONGED TO ANDY
WARHOL AND WAS A GIFT
FROM CHERYL TIEGS. THE
CHANDELIER WAS INSPIRED
BY TONY DUQUETTE.
PREVIOUS PAGES, LEFT: A
FINE EARLY-EIGHTEENTH-
CENTURY JEWELER'S
CABINET OF EBONY INLAID
WITH IVORY SITS IN MY
DINING ROOM. IT NOW
HOUSES MY SILVERWARE
AND NAPKIN RING
COLLECTION. ON TOP IS A
COLLECTION OF CORALS. THE
MIDDLE ONE WAS FOUND IN
AN ANTIQUE STORE ON CAPRI.
RIGHT: ORCHIDS ARE
DISPLAYED IN ANTIQUE
DECANTERS ON THE MANTEL.
THE ERODED BUST IS
ROMAN, AND BEHIND IT IS
A SEVENTEENTH-CENTURY
PERUVIAN GILDED MIRROR.

TOP LEFT: **I USED OLD WORLD WEAVERS TOILE FOR A GUEST BEDROOM.** TOP RIGHT: **AN EIGHTEENTH-CENTURY TIBETAN MONK SITS WATCH ON AN ITALIAN PRAYER CHEST.** CENTER RIGHT: **THE KITCHEN STILL RETAINS ITS ORIGINAL O'KEEFE AND MERRITT COOKER.** BOTTOM RIGHT: **ANTIQUE FRENCH APOTHECARY JARS ON OPEN SHELVING IN THE KITCHEN.** BOTTOM LEFT: **A TABLE SET FOR AFTERNOON TEA IN MY GARDEN PAVILION, WITH NINETEENTH-CENTURY BAVARIAN GLASS, EIGHTEENTH-CENTURY CHINESE GILDED BRONZE DEITIES, AND 1940S FRENCH PORCELAIN.** OPPOSITE: **THE BREAKFAST NOOK IS HUNG WITH MEXICAN AND SOUTH AMERICAN RETABLOS. THE BENCH IS PORTUGUESE AND THE TABLE MID-NINETEENTH-CENTURY INDIAN.**

ABOVE: I AM PASSIONATE ABOUT PHOTOGRAPHY AND
DISPLAY MY COLLECTION THROUGHOUT MY HOME AND
OFFICE. IN THE LIBRARY ARE SOME OF MY FAVORITES
BY SUCH ARTISTS AS PETER BEARD, YUL BRYNNER, PAT
YORK, HERB RITTS, JEAN COCTEAU, AND CINDY SHERMAN.
THE ANTIQUE FRENCH LEATHER SOFA HAS A NEW LARSON
SILK VELVET SEAT. THE VICTORIAN IRON ROCKING CHAIR
IS FROM JF CHEN, AND THE CURTAIN FABRIC IS BY PETER
DUNHAM. LEFT: A DETAIL OF THE ARABESQUE EMBROIDERY
I HAD APPLIED TO THE BOTTOM OF THE SOFA. A
NINETEENTH-CENTURY SYRIAN INLAID WOOD AND MOTHER-
OF-PEARL TABLE ADDS AN EXOTIC ELEMENT. OPPOSITE,
TOP LEFT: A COLLECTION OF ANTIQUE CANDLESTICKS
JUXTAPOSED WITH THE MODERN JEAN-MICHEL BASQUIAT IN
MY LIVING ROOM. TOP RIGHT: A DETAIL OF A SILK-COVERED
BYRON CHAIR. THE PILLOW IS BY RIFAT OZBEK.
BOTTOM: THE BOLD COLOR PALETTE OF THE LIVING ROOM
IS FRAMED BY RED SILK DAMASK CURTAINS. AN OLIVE
GREEN STRIPED SILK FROM SCHUMACHER WAS USED TO
COVER LARGE, RECTANGULAR PILLOWS FOR THE SOFA. THE
CHEST IS EIGHTEENTH-CENTURY PORTUGUESE, AND THE
COFFEE TABLE IS A REPRODUCTION FROM MY LINE. THE
VINTAGE MOROCCAN RUG FROM MANSOUR MODERN SITS
ON THE RECLAIMED WALNUT FLOORS FROM EXQUISITE
SURFACES. PREVIOUS PAGES, LEFT: GLORIA SWANSON'S
CHANDELIER STILL HANGS IN THE DINING ROOM, BUT I
ADDED TURKISH CANDLE BURNERS FOR MORE DRAMA.
THE CEILING STENCIL WAS TAKEN FROM A FABRIC I
FOUND IN VENICE. THE ITALIAN TABLE AND CHAIRS
MATCH MY COLLECTION OF MILANESE INLAID EBONY AND
IVORY FURNITURE. RIGHT: A DETAIL OF AN EIGHTEENTH-
CENTURY CHAIR IN FRONT OF THE DRAPES MADE FROM
MY MAJORELLE LINEN PRINT. BEYOND IS THE HOUSE'S
ORIGINAL MALIBU TILE FOUNTAIN.

ABOVE: MY BEDSIDE TABLE IS COVERED IN
OBJECTS THAT I LOVE: A SILVER-COVERED
RUSSIAN ICON FRAMED IN BLOND TORTOISE
SHELL THAT I BOUGHT ON MY FIRST TRIP TO
ISTANBUL; A BRONZE RODIN SCULPTURE OF PUCK;
A SEVENTEENTH-CENTURY ITALIAN SANGUINE
DRAWING OF A SATYR; AN INDIAN SILVER BOX;
AND A MAHARAJAH'S EMBLEM OF THREE LIONS
IN SILVER REPOUSSÉ. VINTAGE PHOTOS OF MY
MOTHER AND GRANDMOTHER AS YOUNG GIRLS
ADD A PERSONAL NOTE. LEFT: THE ORIGINAL ART
DECO BATHROOM WAS ENHANCED BY ADDING
SLIGHTLY AGED MIRROR AND VENETIAN PLASTER
TO THE WALLS AND CEILING. THE MISSONI TOWELS
AND MANUEL CANOVAS SHOWER CURTAIN FABRIC
ADD A FUN MODERN ELEMENT. OPPOSITE: MY
PORTUGUESE BED IS THE EIGHTEENTH-CENTURY
ORIGINAL THAT INSPIRED ME TO PUT THE LISBON
BED INTO MY FURNITURE LINE. THE LEATHER-
STUDDED CHEST IS LATE-SEVENTEENTH-CENTURY
SPANISH. HERE, IN WINTER, THE BED IS DRESSED
IN ANTIQUE SCOTTISH PAISLEYS, BUT IN THE
SUMMER I REPLACE THEM WITH COLORFUL BATIK
PRINTS FROM BALI AND IKATS FROM UZBEKISTAN.

Piano Man's Pad

SIR ELTON JOHN AND DAVID FURNISH'S HIP HOLLYWOOD HOME

Elton has had a love/hate relationship with L.A. He debuted his U.S. career at the legendary Troubadour in the 1970s and went on to own several Beverly Hills mansions over the years. But a decade ago he abandoned the city and stayed at the Beverly Hills Hotel when in L.A. for concerts or his famous Oscar parties.

During a delicious stay at the Castel Mont Alban, Elton and David's villa on the Côte d'Azur (which I have nicknamed the "healing house," due to its incredible spa-like qualities), David asked me to help them find an apartment in L.A. so they could spend more time there, have a real home base, and create a sanctuary for Elton when playing in Las Vegas.

So I set about the task, found a three-bedroom apartment (which we converted into one, with large rock-star–style closets and an open plan for easy living/ entertaining, and have since expanded with the addition of baby Zachary), and together David and I designed a spectacular home for them both. (Elton, in fact, saw the apartment only the day he bought it and didn't go back until the day I had finished it.) It was a dream job. Elton and David let me run free with color and texture, even flying me around the world to visit all their homes (including two in England, a palazzo in Venice, a museum-size apartment in Atlanta, and the villa in the South of France) so I could choose art to include in my decorative scheme. David loves modernism and wanted to make the feel of the apartment match the period of the building. So with the directive of Studio 54, Halston chic, and Hermès Kelly-bag green, I designed for them what Elton now refers to as his "floating jewel box."

OPPOSITE: SIR ELTON JOHN, CBE, AND DAVID FURNISH AT HOME IN FRONT OF A DAMIEN HIRST COLOR WHEEL PAINTING. PREVIOUS PAGES: A SECOND-CENTURY A.D. ROMAN BUST IS JUXTAPOSED AGAINST THE L.A. SKYLINE. IN THIS COZY SITTING CORNER DOMINATED BY A WANG GUANGYI PAINTING, THE COUPLE RELAXES AND WATCHES MOVIES. THE CUSTOM-BUILT COFFEE TABLE SLIDES OPEN TO REVEAL A FULLY STOCKED MIRRORED BAR INSIDE.

"We wanted something very '70s L.A.-inspired, à la Boogie Nights."
—ELTON JOHN

ABOVE: A DAMIAN HIRST SPIN PAINTING ADDS VIBRANT COLOR TO THE DINING ROOM. THE 1960S ITALIAN ART GLASS TIES IN THE COLORS. **OPPOSITE, TOP LEFT:** SCULPTURES BY DALE CHIHULY AND MARC QUINN SIT AGAINST THE SKYLINE. **TOP RIGHT:** ELTON'S OFFICE WALLS ARE COVERED IN BRONZE LEATHER. HIS CHAIR IS COVERED IN CUSTOM DYED ALLIGATOR. **BOTTOM:** A KEITH HARING OIL PAINTING DOMINATES THE WALL OF THE LIVING ROOM AND SPARKLES OFF THE GREEN VENETIAN GALICE PLASTER WALLS.
PREVIOUS PAGES: IN THE LIVING ROOM, A MINOTTI SOFA IS PAIRED WITH BARCELONA CHAIRS AND A LIME GREEN SUEDE-COVERED CHAISE. ON THE CUSTOM-MADE ONYX COFFEE TABLES (WHICH ARE LIT FROM WITHIN AT NIGHT) SIT VENETIAN GLASS ITEMS FROM ELTON'S COLLECTION AS WELL AS A STERLING SILVER DAMIEN HIRST EXPLODING SKULL SCULPTURE.

THE POLIFORM KITCHEN
IS CREAM LACQUER WITH
CHOCOLATE CAESARSTONE
COUNTERTOPS. THE
CHANDELIER HANGING
OVER THE ISLAND IS BY
SEGUSO, CIRCA 1960,
AND ONCE HUNG IN THE
LOBBY OF THE GRAND
HOTEL, MILAN. ELTON AND
DAVID HAVE A PASSION
FOR ART GLASS, SO I FELT
THIS FIXTURE WOULD
GIVE THEIR KITCHEN A
PERSONAL TOUCH. THE
ISLAND DIVIDES THE LIVING
SPACE AND CREATES A
COMFORTABLE SPOT
FOR BREAKFAST AND
CASUAL MEETINGS.

ABOVE: THE GALLERY LEADS TO THE COUPLE'S MASTER SUITE. THE WALLS ARE LINED WITH COLOR PHOTOGRAPHS BY WILLIAM EGGLESTON AND WILLIAM CLAXTON. TWO 1960S WORKS ON PAPER BY WILLEM DE KOONING ARE ON THE LEFT WALL. LEFT: WARHOL "FRIGHT WIG" IMAGES GRACE THE WALLS OF THE BATHROOM. OPPOSITE, TOP LEFT: IN ELTON'S CLOSET, A KALEIDOSCOPIC ARRAY OF TOM FORD SILK ROBES AND VELVET SLIPPERS. TOP RIGHT: A VINTAGE PIERRE PAULIN RIBBON CHAIR, BOUGHT AT L.A.'S FAMOUS FASHION STORE MAXFIELD, IS UPHOLSTERED IN RED SUEDE. WHITING & DAVIS SILVER METAL MESH WAS USED AS SHEERS FOR THE MASTER BEDROOM. BOTTOM LEFT: A 1960S MURANO FIXTURE HIGHLIGHTS THE WHITE GOLD AND MARBLE BISAZZA TILE MOSAIC IN THE BATHROOM. BOTTOM RIGHT: A DAVID LACHAPELLE *LIZ TAYLOR* IN THE POWDER ROOM WITH MAYA ROMANOFF MURANO GLASS BEAD WALLPAPER. VINTAGE VENINI GLASS VASES ARE GROUPED TOGETHER UNDER THE CUSTOM-DESIGNED SINK UNIT.

THE BED IS UPHOLSTERED IN PYTHON SKIN AND COVERED IN A PAUL RENWICK SHAVED MINK BLANKET. CUSTOM EMBROIDERED SHEETS ARE FROM FRETTE. THE CHOCOLATE GALICE WALLS ARE THE PERFECT BACKDROP FOR THE TRACY EMIN NEON SCULPTURE. ON THE B & B ITALIA SIDE TABLES SIT 1960s LAMPS BY AMERICAN SCULPTOR CURTIS JERE. THE GARY HUME PAINTING GIVES AN UNEXPECTED BURST OF COLOR TO THIS SEXY ROOM.

Casa Aramara

Y ou would never expect this notorious client of mine to live in such great style, but Joe Francis of the much-talked-about *Girls Gone Wild* has a passion for life that is only amplified by his passion for perfection in all that he does, and that includes his homes. Over the years we have worked on five of them (plus a G-force jet), but the jewel in his real estate crown is his forty-thousand-square-foot estate in Punta Mita, Mexico. The Casa Aramara has become a heavenly respite from his busy life running Mantra Films, Perfect Skin for the Kardashians, and numerous other enterprises. But this extraordinary villa, which I oversaw with my original company from ground up and recently gave a new spin using fabrics from my eponymous line, has also become the playground of Joe's friends and business associates. Joe has been uncommonly generous with loaning the house out to such glitterati as Hollywood über-agent Kevin Huvane, president of Hearst Entertainment Scott Sassa, musicians Quincy Jones and Jennifer Lopez, and actresses Jennifer Aniston, Courteney Cox, Kim Kardashian, and Paris Hilton.

It was a difficult project from the start, fighting monsoons, humidity, extreme heat, and mosquitoes with an irregular crew. But fight through it we did, and today the tropical beauty of the Palupa architecture and the luxurious interiors make you feel like you have been transported to paradise. We shopped the world for furnishings, had items custom-made in Bali and Jakarta, and imported treasures from the South Seas and other Dutch colonies. Artwork was collected to punch up the decor. The overall vibe is set for complete relaxation, sexy lounging, and dancing the night away, with guacamole in bowls, margaritas in hand, and sand between your toes.

OPPOSITE: THE PATHWAY THAT LEADS TO THE ENTRANCE OF THE ESTATE IS PAVED IN MEXICAN MARBLE. THE COLUMNS HAVE PEBBLE-WORK MOSAICS INLAID INTO THE PLASTER. MULTI-POINTED STAR LANTERNS WERE CUSTOM-MADE FOR THE PROJECT IN THIS HUGE SCALE BY REBORN ANTIQUES. PREVIOUS PAGES: THE SWEEPING POOL WAS DESIGNED TO TIE IN WITH THE SHAPE OF THE BEACH DIRECTLY IN FRONT OF IT. THE TEAK LOUNGERS WERE CUSTOM-DESIGNED AND MADE IN BALI. WHITE TOWELING SLIPCOVERS AND BATIK PILLOWS LEND AN AIR OF LUXURY.

ABOVE: THE "CABINET OF CURIOSITIES" IS INDO-COLONIAL FROM THE EARLY NINETEENTH CENTURY. THE WALL DESIGN WAS TAKEN FROM AN ANTIQUE INDONESIAN DOCUMENT AND HAND-PAINTED BY KELLY HOLDEN. **RIGHT:** THE MASSIVE DINING ROOM TABLE IS THIRTY FEET LONG AND MADE FROM ONE TREE TRUNK. THE CHAIRS ARE COVERED IN MY MAMOUNIA FABRIC. **PREVIOUS PAGES:** THE VAST LIVING ROOM IS GROUNDED BY AN INDIAN FLAT-WEAVE RUG I DESIGNED FOR MANSOUR MODERN. THE CHAIRS AND PILLOWS WERE COVERED IN KABA KABA AND SENJA FROM MY FABRIC COLLECTION.

ABOVE: SACRED INDONESIAN TOTEMS ARE ARRANGED AROUND A GROUPING OF PALM TREES THAT ENHANCE THE VIEW OF THE GULF OF MEXICO. THE SMALL BUT CHARMING PUNTA MITA PORT CAN BE SEEN IN THE DISTANCE. EACH COLUMN IS LIT FROM THE GROUND WITH A SMALL SPOTLIGHT SO AT NIGHT THE TOTEMS GLOW AS IF THE MOONLIGHT WERE UPON THEM. **LEFT:** A CARVED INDONESIAN HEAD PRESIDES OVER THE DINING TABLE IN THE POOL HOUSE, A SHADED SPOT FOR LAZY LUNCHES. **OPPOSITE, TOP:** ARRANGED WITH ABANDON UNDER THE PALM TREES IS A TRIO OF DEDON CIRCULAR CHAISES SCATTERED WITH WHITE SUNBRELLA-COVERED PILLOWS, PERFECT FOR AN AFTERNOON SNOOZE. THE LARGE URN IS AN ANCIENT BALINESE WATER VESSEL MADE OF LAVA STONE. **BOTTOM:** THE TEAK TABLETOP HAS AN ANTIQUE STONE WHEEL AS ITS BASE. THE SENJA LINEN PILLOWS AND BATIK-PAINTED PLATES CREATE A TRANQUIL SETTING FOR BREAKFAST OVERLOOKING THE OCEAN.

ABOVE: IN THE GARDEN HOUSE THE TRADITIONAL-STYLE BUILT-IN SOFA IS CASUALLY SCATTERED WITH CHEERFUL PILLOWS. THE CARVED PANELS ON THE WALL ARE FROM BALI, WHILE THE BRONZE HORSEMAN SCULPTURE BY A LOCAL ARTIST WAS FOUND IN PUERTO VALLARTA. RIGHT: AN ANTIQUE MEXICAN DOOR WAS TURNED INTO A COFFEE TABLE, AND THE DEEP CLUB CHAIR WAS UPHOLSTERED IN MY BODRUM STRIPE LINEN. THE MOROCCAN INLAID SIDE TABLE CAME FROM HOLLYHOCK, L.A., AND THE CERAMIC PINEAPPLE LAMP IS VINTAGE. FOLLOWING PAGE: THE GAME ROOM IS DOMINATED BY A FULL-SIZE POOL TABLE. PETER BEARD DIARY PAGES LEAD THE EYE TO THE SOARING PALAPA ROOF.

ABOVE: TIE-DYED RICE PAPER LINES THE WALLS OF A POWDER ROOM. A VINTAGE IRON BENCH FOUND IN PARIS IS UPHOLSTERED IN A RAOUL TEXTILE, AND AFRICAN BOWLS DRESS UP THE LIMESTONE COUNTERTOP. RIGHT: THIS BEDROOM HAS AN UPHOLSTERED HEADBOARD AND PILLOWS IN MY MARRAKESH FABRIC, AND THE 1930S TEAK PLANTER'S CHAIRS WERE COVERED IN TURKISH TICKING. THE TRIBAL-INSPIRED RUG WAS MADE BY MANSOUR MODERN.

A Collector's Eye

Hal Levitt must have been one of the most talented, yet unheralded architects in America. His amazing houses range from mid-century marvels like the Vidal Sassoon house to more unusual structures like the Dirks/Dougherty residence located in the heart of Bel Air, with its lofty ceilings, extraordinary log beams, and spacious rooms.

I fell into this job because the client, Carolyn, had seen a house I had decorated for some neighbors, a young family with two small children. She called me immediately, praising the home and asking if I could create a twist on it for the home she shares with her husband, Brett. The couple had bought furniture that completely didn't match the style of the architecture, and I had to gently tell them I could not work with it. I could, however, work with the antique pieces that they had inherited and bought over the years. Slowly they donated all the inappropriate furnishings to St. Mary's Hospice, and we set about scouring the world for the finest examples of Italian, Portuguese, and Swedish furniture from the seventeenth and eighteenth centuries. To my surprise, Carolyn has a connoisseur's eye and allowed me to educate her in fine furniture and decorative items: Georgian silver, rare tortoise-shell–inlay pieces, Han dynasty pottery and terra-cotta, ivory Vizagapatam penwork boxes, and very fine Impressionist art.

I brought in from Paris a master dealer, Patricia Marshall, who helped us secure museum-quality pieces, mostly from private collections, by Picasso (Blue Period), Bonnard, Marquet, Degas, Pissarro, Modigliani, Giacometti, and Vuillard.

OPPOSITE: AN IMPORTANT BLUE PERIOD PICASSO PAINTING SITS ABOVE AN EIGHTEENTH-CENTURY IVORY-INLAID TABLE IN THE ENTRY. A HAN DYNASTY TERRA-COTTA HORSE IS BALANCED BY PAINTED AND LACQUERED CHINESE TRUNKS. **PREVIOUS PAGES, LEFT:** THE ENTRY TO THE HOUSE WAS DESIGNED BY ARCHITECT HAL LEVITT IN THE 1950S. **RIGHT:** A DETAIL OF THE LIVING ROOM COFFEE TABLE SHOWS A HAN DYNASTY VASE JUXTAPOSED WITH A PICASSO CERAMIC JUG.

Having had a career in fashion, Carolyn was also open to collecting fashion photography for her office (which contains a spectacular desk that once belonged to Karl X, King of Sweden). Working with the great David Fahey (who also started Elton John's photography collection), we bought masterworks from William Klein, Herb Ritts, Richard Avedon, Melvin Sokolsky, Cecil Beaton, and Man Ray.

Today the collection is a varied mix of fine furniture, quirky charismatic accessories, and cherry-picked artworks, all of which blend perfectly into a very relaxed setting and match the easy-going nature of this couple. Together we became educated in Impressionism and had untold fun hunting down rare works and traveling to Paris and London to inspect the pieces. It taught me much about important furniture and how to mix artwork of many periods to create decorative harmony and visual balance.

THE FAMILY ROOM COLORS WERE PULLED FROM THIS FINE ZIEGLER MAHAL RUG AND ARE COMPLEMENTED BY A TRIPTYCH BY JOE GOODE. FAUX-BOIS FABRIC PILLOWS FROM MY COLLECTION DRESS THE SOFA. THE COFFEE TABLE WAS MADE FROM AN EIGHTEENTH-CENTURY ITALIAN CENTER TABLE FOUND AT BONHAMS & BUTTERFIELDS AUCTION, AND THE RED LACQUER ARMOIRE IS MING DYNASTY. THE VENETIAN GROTTO STOOL WAS ADDED AS A WHIMSICAL TOUCH.

ABOVE: DOMINATING THE DINING ROOM IS A PAIR OF PAINTINGS DEPICTING BEHIND-THE-SCENES VIEWS OF THE MOULIN ROUGE BY RENOWNED FRENCH PAINTER ÉDOUARD VUILLARD. I FOUND THE CAPTAIN'S TABLE AND QUEEN ANNE CHAIRS IN LONDON.

OPPOSITE: THE GUISEPPE GALLO PAINTING OVER THE MANTEL BRINGS BOLD COLOR INTO THE BEDROOM. THE EIGHTEENTH-CENTURY VENETIAN CHAIR WAS MADE FOR A GONDOLA, AND THE TOILE TABLE CAME FROM THE JACK WARNER ESTATE. PREVIOUS PAGES: A VIEW OF THE LIVING ROOM WITH PIERRE BONNARD'S *CHIEN CHASSANT DES OISEAUX* AND TWO DRAWINGS BY MODIGLIANI AND DEGAS.

OPPOSITE, TOP FROM LEFT: ROSES IN A HAN DYNASTY BOWL SIT BESIDE A FABERGÉ AGATE DISH. A PISSARRO HANGS ABOVE AN EIGHTEENTH-CENTURY PORTUGUESE TOOLED LEATHER SETTEE. AN OPEN *SECRETAIRE* REVEALS CLOISONNÉ MELON DISHES AND A FIFTEENTH-CENTURY BUDDHA HEAD. CENTER FROM LEFT: A PICASSO VASE HOLDS PEONIES IN THE BEDROOM. EBONY AND IVORY ARTISTS' MODELS SIT ON A REGENCY TABLE. ROGERS & GOFFIGON LINEN AND MY MARRAKESH PILLOW DRESS A CLUB CHAIR IN THE LIVING ROOM. BOTTOM FROM LEFT: A DETAIL OF FINE INDIAN PAISLEY ON A SEVENTEENTH-CENTURY ITALIAN CHAIR. CENTER: AN EIGHTEENTH-CENTURY ITALIAN CHEST HOLDS HAN DYNASTY VASES. A LARGE SIXTEENTH-CENTURY DUTCH MIRROR REFLECTS AN EIGHTEENTH-CENTURY CHANDELIER FROM PIEDMONT, ITALY. ABOVE: THE OFFICE WALLS ARE COVERED IN PHOTOGRAPHS BY HERB RITTS, RICHARD AVEDON, HORST P. HORST, CECIL BEATON, AND MELVIN SOKOLSKY. THE DESK ONCE BELONGED TO KING KARL X OF SWEDEN.

ABOVE: AN EIGHTEENTH-CENTURY PORTUGUESE JACARANDA WOOD CABINET HOUSES A COLLECTION OF PICASSO CERAMICS DEPICTING FACES, WHILE NINETEENTH-CENTURY SANG DE BOEUF VASES ON TOP ADD HEIGHT AND COLOR. THE ALLIGATOR-COVERED ARMCHAIRS ARE WILLIAM IV. OPPOSITE: IN THE MASTER BEDROOM, A RARE DUTCH OLIVE WOOD MIRROR ONCE OWNED BY BABE PALEY SITS ON LIME-WASHED OAK PLANK WALLS. AN EIGHTEENTH-CENTURY ITALIAN COMMODE ACTS AS A BEDSIDE TABLE ON TOP OF WHICH RESTS A SKETCH BY TOULOUSE-LAUTREC. THE BED IS COVERED IN NINETEENTH-CENTURY PAISLEY SHAWLS AND FRETTE LINENS.

World Tour

Thee first time I met Cher was in her bedroom. It has since been the site of many meetings but was unexpected for my first. Upon arriving at her spectacular Malibu manse—which resembles a cross between the Alhambra and the historic Danieli Hotel in Venice—I was immediately ushered up a larger-than-life staircase that Gloria Swanson herself would have been proud to descend, ready for her close-up. Through heavily studded dark walnut Gothic doors I was guided into a room hung with Victorian Orientalist paintings and furnished with heavy Pugin-style pieces. Through a beautiful Andalusian archway Cher appeared. Radiant in sterling-silver–studded jeans, long diamond-encrusted feather earrings, and a turquoise silk camisole, the award-winning actress and pop icon greeted me in her personal retreat and explained that she wanted to freshen up her life via her interior. Surprisingly shy and intensely private, she needed her home to be her castle, her special meditative place, and her sanctuary. I was mesmerized by her intense love of all things design and her constant striving for perfection.

Over the next few months we established that the way to lighten, brighten, and refresh this palazzo was to banish all things Gothic (as magnificent and rare as her collection was) and reinvent the home as a Moorish-style villa. We organized a (now-legendary) auction and set about searching the world for fine examples of Orientalist furnishings, particularly Moroccan and Egyptian decorative items, accessorized with Indonesian artifacts and beautiful seventeenth- and

OPPOSITE: THE ENTRANCE TO CHER'S PERSONAL PARADISE. PREVIOUS PAGES: THE VIEW FROM CHER'S FAMILY ROOM ACROSS THE POOL AND OUT TO POINT DUME, MALIBU. A GIANT STONE BUDDHA GUARDS OVER ALL. THE MARBLE BALUSTRADES CAME FROM WILLIAM RANDOLPH HEARST'S SAN SIMEON.

"I never get tired of coming into these beautiful, peaceful rooms." — CHER

eighteenth-century Guan Yin sculptures from Asian temples. I shopped for her in every country I visited over the course of the next five years, and together we created a beautiful, tranquil new interior. Still a work in progress (as Cher takes great pains to make sure the finished product is very personal to her aesthetic), the home now sparkles as a fresh and creative space. Having spent the last three Christmases there with Cher and her closest family members and friends, I have enjoyed firsthand the magic that lives in the air in this home and sanctuary.

ABOVE LEFT: VENETIAN-STYLE WINDOWS WITH LEADED GLASS LOOK OUT TO THE MOROCCAN COURTYARD. **ABOVE RIGHT:** A CORDED SILK UPHOLSTERED CHAISE FACES UNINTERRUPTED OCEAN VIEWS FROM CHER'S BEDROOM. **OPPOSITE:** THIS INTIMATE NOOK LEADS DOWN TO THE SCREENING ROOM. AN INDIAN BENCH IS COVERED IN SILK BURLAP. THE MOROCCAN TABLE IS INLAID WITH SILVER REPOUSSÉ WORK. **FOLLOWING PAGES:** THE WALLS OF CHER'S PRIVATE SITTING ROOM ARE COVERED IN RAW SCHUMACHER SILK THAT WAS CUSTOM-STENCILED ON SITE TO LOOK LIKE INDIAN WEDDING HENNA. THE SOFAS FOR THIS SPACE WERE CUSTOM-MADE IN AN ORIENTAL MANNER. THE CHINESE TABLE IS EARLY EIGHTEENTH CENTURY.

OPPOSITE: THE TIN CEILING IN THE DINING ROOM WAS PAINTED ANTIQUE WHITE. THE BRASS LANTERNS WERE SHIPPED FROM TANGIER. THE WALL SCONCES WERE MADE FROM LANTERNS I FOUND IN ISTANBUL, AND THE MOROCCAN-STYLE DINING CHAIRS ARE COVERED IN PALE SAGE SHAGREEN. **ABOVE:** A SEVENTEENTH-CENTURY CHINESE ELM CONSOLE SHELTERS ANCIENT BUDDHAS AND MONKS FROM TIBET. ON TOP IS A GROUPING OF SILVER ETHIOPIAN CROSSES.

TOP FROM LEFT: AN EGYPTIAN-REVIVAL VASE FROM CHER'S "EGYPTIAN PERIOD." GOLD-LEAF CEILINGS IN THE LIVING ROOM WERE HAND-PAINTED BY BRAD SOUTHWICK. TEA-STAINED STENCILED SILK WALLS LEAD TO CHER'S DRESSING ROOM. CENTER FROM LEFT: THE STONE BUDDHA IS EIGHT FEET TALL. CHER'S SYRIAN BED HAS SILK EMBROIDERED ANICHINI PILLOWS. THE INNER COURTYARD. BOTTOM FROM LEFT: A VAST PIERCED-BRASS LANTERN HANGS AGAINST BLEACHED CEILING BEAMS IN THE ENTRY. A CARVED WOODEN BUDDHA SITS IN FRONT OF AN ANTIQUE INDONESIAN ARCHITECTURAL PANEL IN THE FAMILY ROOM.

ABOVE: CHER'S SYRIAN MOTHER-OF-PEARL–INLAID BED, WHICH I BOUGHT AT AN MGM STUDIOS AUCTION, ONCE BELONGED TO VALENTINO'S WIFE, NATACHA RAMBOVA. THE BEDSIDE LAMPS ARE NINETEENTH-CENTURY EGYPTIAN BRASS INLAID WITH SILVER AND COPPER. THE SILK DUPIONI "ONION" SHADE IS A FAVORITE STYLE OF CHER'S. PREVIOUS PAGE: AN INDIAN DAY BED IS COVERED IN CORRAGIO PAISLEY CHENILLE. TWO NINETEENTH-CENTURY INDIAN ELEPHANT PROCESSIONAL DRUMS ACT AS COLUMNS TO HOLD

Out of Africa

CHRIS CORTAZZO'S MAGICAL MALIBU RANCH

I met Chris Cortazzo at an Oscar lunch honoring my friend Tamara Mellon about seven years ago, and we ended up seeing each other at every Oscar event that week. So by the end of it we felt like the oldest of friends, and we have now traveled the world together, from trips on super yachts to such heavenly Mediterranean jewels as Portofino, to rubbing shoulders with movie stars and royalty in exclusive St. Tropez villas, to a South African safari on Elton John's yearly ritual to the Royal Malawian estate. Yet we have just as much fun sharing a veggie burger (Chris is a vegan) in the hole-in-the-wall organic cafe on Melrose Avenue in West Hollywood. So it was a pleasure to help Chris transform his property into a dream home tailored especially for him.

Chris is a successful realtor specializing in properties on the legendary Malibu coastline, yet when it came to buying his own dream hideaway, he chose a twenty-seven-acre plot in the Malibu Hills without even an ocean view. However, it has ravishing grounds and breathtaking undulating mountain backdrops.

The original house was a small, Spanish cabin-style building with a series of odd outbuildings and garages. We wanted to transform the house into a one-bedroom master suite, with comfortable surroundings that matched the outside vista. Enormous metal-framed windows were installed to flood in light and take in the striking panorama and babbling brook. Beautiful reclaimed French oak was used for the floors and cabinetry, and eco-friendly devices were used wherever possible, from water-saving toilets, graywater irrigation systems, and energy-saving electrical appliances.

Comfort was key. We chose deep slipcovered club-style sofas and armchairs, as well as plush tribal Moroccan and Afghani rugs that add texture underfoot

OPPOSITE: THE STACKED-STONE FIREPLACE DISPLAYS A COLLECTION OF ANTIQUE AFRICAN CURRENCY AND PHOTOGRAPHY BY HERB RITTS AND RICHARD GERE. PREVIOUS PAGES: THE LIVING ROOM IS DOMINATED BY THREE LENI RIEFENSTAHL VINTAGE AFRICAN PHOTOGRAPHS PURCHASED AT THE FAHEY/KLEIN GALLEY. A NINETEENTH-CENTURY RUSTIC WELSH LADDER CHAIR SITS IN THE CORNER, WHILE AN AXEL VERVOORDT COFFEE TABLE SITS ON A TURN-OF-THE-LAST-CENTURY BERBER TRIBAL RUG.

OPPOSITE: A PETER BEARD PHOTOGRAPH WITH "KUMANTE" ADORNMENT IS A FOCAL POINT IN THE MASTER BEDROOM. THE FOLDING BENCH IS FROM GREGORIUS PINEO. ABOVE: THE CAPTAIN'S TABLE IS SURROUNDED BY RALPH LAUREN CHAIRS. A CUSTOM RAFFIA SHADE HANGS ON A BRONZE CHAIN ABOVE. THE FLOORING IS RECLAIMED FRENCH WHITE OAK FROM NIKZAD. THE CANDLESTICKS WERE BOUGHT FROM ANTIQUE MARKETS AROUND LONDON WHILE ON A SHOPPING TRIP WITH CHRIS JUST BEFORE I INSTALLED THE INTERIORS. THE PHOTOGRAPHY ON THE LEFT WALL BY HERB RITTS WAS PART OF HIS AFRICA SERIES FROM THE FAHEY/KLEIN GALLERY.

while retaining a masculine air. To personalize the home we started collecting African-inspired art and artifacts. Photography is Chris's passion, and important works by Peter Beard, Nick Brandt, and Herb Ritts can be found throughout the estate. We anchored the collection with three iconic works of mammoth scale by Leni Riefenstahl that balance the high-vaulted living room ceilings.

The rest of the property now features three guesthouses decorated in a whimsical style that mixes British colonial furnishings and fun colored textiles with the African-inspired collections. They have become a favorite spot for friends and family members to spend relaxed weekends and completely rejuvenate. Cooking, swimming, hiking, and laughing are the preferred pastimes of this estate. Thanksgiving is particularly special: Tofurky in abundance, lashings of organic veggies, and more hilarity than you can take.

ABOVE: THE PRIVATE SITTING ROOM ADJOINS THE MASTER BEDROOM AND IS FURNISHED WITH A VINTAGE LEATHER CHESTERFIELD AND A COFFEE TABLE, BOTH FROM MECOX GARDENS. THE RUG IS A 1920S AFGHAN DHURRIE, AND THE GREEN-WARE CHINA IS EARLY NINETEENTH CENTURY. **OPPOSITE:** IN THE SUNROOM, LOGS ARE STORED IN METAL- AND BRASS-STUDDED CABINETS I DESIGNED SPECIALLY FOR THE SPACE. THE NINETEENTH-CENTURY INDIAN ROSEWOOD TABLE WAS FOUND AT AN ANTIQUES STORE ON DUANE STREET IN NEW YORK. THE LION PHOTOGRAPHS ARE BY HERB RITTS AND NICK BRANDT. CHRIS AND I FOUND THE AFRICAN HEADRESTS THAT SIT ON THE MANTEL WHILE ON SAFARI IN SOUTH AFRICA.

ABOVE: NICK BRANDT PHOTOGRAPHS GIVE AN AFRICAN VIBE TO CHRIS'S MOTHER'S ROOM. ON THE BED IS A TURKISH HORSE BLANKET. **TOP RIGHT:** *LORIKEE WITH SPEAR* BY HERB RITTS IS FRAMED BY THE POSTS OF THE MASTER BED. **LEFT:** A BYRON CHAIR IS COVERED IN BODRUM STRIPE. **RIGHT:** SULTAN'S GARDEN FABRIC WALLS IN A GUESTHOUSE. **BOTTOM LEFT:** AN ECLECTIC MIX OF OBJECTS IS GROUNDED BY THE NICK BRANDT PHOTOGRAPHS. **BOTTOM RIGHT:** NATURAL SCHUMACHER BELGIAN LINEN DRESSES THE WINDOWS OF THE CARRARA-MARBLE–WAINSCOTED MASTER BATHROOM. **OPPOSITE:** THE TIMOTHY BED FROM MY FURNITURE COLLECTION WAS EBONIZED TO GIVE CONTRAST IN A GUESTHOUSE. HERB RITTS PHOTOGRAPHS HANG IN MY FATIMA FRAMES. THE ANTIQUE INDIAN TEXTILES ARE FROM GUINEVERE IN LONDON, AND THE SEAGRASS RUG IS FROM POTTERY BARN.

ABOVE: THE SPLENDID GARDENS OF THE RANCH ARE LIKE A MAGICAL LAND. THEY FEEL VERY "ALICE IN WONDERLAND" WITH THEIR VAST TEAK-FRAMED OPERA SOFA MADE FOR ME BY POSSE UPHOLSTERY AND COVERED IN A PERENNIALS STRIPE. THE WINGED TEAK CHAIRS GIVE THE ANTIQUE TEAK OUTDOOR DINING TABLE AN ADDED FEELING OF WHIMSY.

FOLLOWING PAGES, TOP LEFT: THE EIGHTEEN-FOOT CURVED SOFA PROVIDES SEXY SEATING TO WATCH MOVIES OUTDOORS. BOTTOM LEFT: HIDDEN BEHIND A SHRUB, THE POOL IS REVEALED AS A SURPRISE TO GUESTS WHO ENTER THROUGH THE CARVED-OUT ARCH IN THE BUSHES. TOP CENTER: ME AND CHRIS CORTAZZO OUTSIDE THE MAIN HOUSE. TOP RIGHT: THE OPERA SOFA. BOTTOM RIGHT: THE POOL HOUSE IS FURNISHED WITH DEEP SOFAS AND A TELEVISION. A WOOD-BURNING FIREPLACE MAKES FOR COZY EVENINGS POOLSIDE.

Greystone

THE LEGENDARY GREYSTONE
MANSION IN BEVERLY HILLS

The Greystone mansion, built in 1924 for the infamous oil-rich Doheny family, was one of the most extravagant estates ever built in Beverly Hills. The original estate sprawled over twenty acres of prime real estate and included hunting grounds, waterfalls, swimming pools, a lake, and a mini golf course. The house itself, now on the National Register of Historic Places of America, is a masterpiece of architecture from that era. The most cutting-edge materials and appliances of the time were used during construction, and treasures were shipped from the four corners of the Earth to enhance the mansion's beauty.

The family fared rather less well than the house, however, and was cursed with murders, betrayals, scandals, and sadness. The house fell into disrepair during the 1960s and was almost demolished in the 1970s after most of its land was sold off and developed. Fortunately, it was saved and now is a national monument. Having appeared in numerous movies and pop videos, and hosted many important events and fundraisers, the house also plays host to events such as the Veranda Great House at Greystone Estate show house. I was lucky enough to be included in this and chose the original gunroom on the first floor as my experiment pad. I launched my first fabric collection here by covering the walls, furniture, and even lampshades in my new designs. I wanted the room to be welcoming and comfortable, yet pay homage to the history and style of this great house.

OPPOSITE: ATOP A PORTUGUESE LIBRARY TABLE SIT CELADON BOWLS FROM FORMATIONS. THE OTTOMAN IS UPHOLSTERED IN EDELMAN LEATHER. **PREVIOUS PAGES:** THE WALLS ARE COVERED IN SULTAN'S GARDEN PAPER-BACKED FABRIC FROM MY OTTOMANIA COLLECTION, WHILE SULTAN'S SUZANI WAS USED FOR THE WINDOW DRAPERY AND QUILTED FOR THE PILLOWS AND BOLSTERS ON THE SOFA. FROM MY FURNITURE COLLECTION ARE BYRON WING CHAIRS, COVERED IN BODRUM STRIPE, AND THE MAHARAJAH COFFEE TABLE. THE VIZAGAPATAM IVORY BOXES ARE EARLY NINETEENTH CENTURY, AND THE USHAK RUG IS FROM MANSOUR.

OPPOSITE: A CANNONBALL CANDLESTICK SITS NEXT TO A VINTAGE AFRICAN MONKEY BOWL. THE LAMP IS 1920S MOROCCAN. TOP LEFT: VELLUM-COVERED BOOKS FROM VOILA LINE THE OLD GUN CASES. TOP RIGHT: THE ORIGINAL NICHES ARE UPHOLSTERED IN SCHUMACHER LINEN, AND CHINESE PORCELAIN FROM CHARLES JACOBSEN IS DISPLAYED ON THE SHELVES. BOTTOM RIGHT: INSPIRED BY AN EIGHTEENTH-CENTURY PORTUGUESE PIECE, THE "LISBON" TABLE WAS DESIGNED FOR THIS ROOM AND IS NOW PART OF MY LINE. THE OTTOMAN IS COVERED IN EDELMAN LEATHER. THE BULLION FRINGE IS FROM HOULES. ABOVE: A NINETEENTH-CENTURY INDIAN WATERCOLOR IN A FINE MOGHUL BRASS, IVORY, AND EBONY-INLAID FRAME.

House of Rock

While vacationing with my friend Diana Jenkins on a boat in the south of France, I witnessed the surprise wedding of Pamela Anderson and Kid Rock. A wild and crazy time ensued, during which the newlyweds asked me to decorate their new love nest in Malibu, California.

Upon returning I set to work, creating a family home for them. Unfortunately, the marriage didn't last, but Kid Rock retained the house and asked me to turn it into a dream bachelor's pad, a place where he could entertain his friends, family, and industry buddies. The space would also accommodate his recording studio, where he would eventually record his number-one hits, "All Summer Long" and "Rock N Roll Jesus."

The home was designed for complete comfort, with easy living areas throughout the house and gardens. Shaded decks and terraces have deep seating in intimate groupings, and lush plantings abound. The mostly white palette of the architecture is balanced by the dark woods of the interior, giving the home its distinctly colonial feeling. The living room is the hub, as Bobby (the nickname for Robert, Kid Rock's real name) uses this room for private jam sessions with friends. It holds a piano that once belonged to Elton John, an important early organ, many guitars, and twin decks for impromptu DJ-ing, another talent of his. To complete the fun, an enormous movie screen descends from the ceiling.

With beautiful Indonesian colonial architecture and interior materials, the home has an air of complete calm and tranquility—somewhat unexpected for a rock star. Kid Rock has grown to love its Zen-like quality as a respite from his hectic touring schedule. The house reflects his character and style, with carefully edited displays of his memorabilia, a photo collection of his musical heroes, and deep, comfortable furniture for lounging, singing, playing guitar, and letting his artistry run free.

OPPOSITE: KID ROCK STANDS IN HIS ENTRYWAY ON A CUSTOM COCONUT GRASS MAT. **PREVIOUS PAGES, LEFT:** A WILLIAM CURTIS ROLF PHOTOGRAPH OF A BABY ELEPHANT IS PLACED ABOVE THE MANTEL IN THE LIVING ROOM. BELOW IS A SELECTION OF KID ROCK'S CUSTOM GUITARS. **RIGHT:** THE FRONT DOOR IS AN ANTIQUE PIECE SALVAGED IN JAVA.

OPPOSITE: A CARVED TEAK BUDDHA WELCOMES GUESTS AT THE ENTRANCE. THE NINETEENTH-CENTURY DUTCH COLONIAL ALTAR CANDLESTICKS ARE FROM JAVA. ABOVE: LEATHER CLUB CHAIRS FROM JEAN DE MERRY AND A CUSTOM WHITE LINEN SLIPCOVERED SOFA CREATE A COZY SEATING AREA IN THE LIVING ROOM. ON THE WALL HANG ANTIQUE INDIAN SITARS AND PHOTOGRAPHS OF ROCK'S FAVORITE MUSICAL IDOLS. PREVIOUS PAGES: A VIEW OF THE HOUSE WITH ITS COLONIAL ARCHITECTURE SEEN FROM THE POOL HOUSE.

OPPOSITE, TOP LEFT: A PORTRAIT OF KID ROCK BECKONS YOU TOWARD HIS MASTER SUITE. TOP RIGHT: A VICTORIAN BENCH FROM RAJASTHAN IS MADE COMFORTABLE WITH A UZBEKISTAN TEXTILE PILLOW. BOTTOM: THE SPACIOUS LIVING ROOM IS FURNISHED FOR EASY LIVING AND CASUAL ENTERTAINING. ASSORTED ANTIQUE BATIK AND TRIBAL FABRIC PILLOWS GIVE CHARACTER TO THE SOFA. ABOVE: A PORTRAIT OF ROCK SITS ABOVE A PRECIOUS 1920S ORGAN. TOP RIGHT: CARVED BALINESE PANELS DISGUISE THE CLOSET. RIGHT: A COPY OF THE TATTOO FROM KID ROCK'S BACK WAS PAINTED ONTO THE FRONT OF THE PIANO, ONCE OWNED BY ELTON JOHN. BELOW: A BRASS-INLAID EIGHTEENTH-CENTURY CHINESE DOOR LEADS TO THE MASTER BEDROOM.

"*There are always people around, eating, drinking, making trouble, or just hanging out. That's what gives this house life.*" —KID ROCK

ABOVE: KID ROCK STRUMS HIS GUITAR ON THE STAIRCASE, WITH A BISON HEAD ABOVE. RIGHT: THE DINING HALL HAS A PHOTO OF CUBA BY MICHAEL EASTMAN. THE DINING TABLE FROM DOS GALLOS WAS MADE FROM AN ANTIQUE FRENCH WINE CELLAR FLOOR. THE NICKEL HANGING FIXTURES ARE FROM URBAN ARCHEOLOGY. FOLLOWING PAGES: THE MODERN KITCHEN HAS A STAINLESS-STEEL ISLAND THAT HOUSES SINKS, A COOKTOP, AND REFRIGERATOR DRAWERS. THE ANTIQUE JEWELERS' STOOLS WERE FOUND IN THE PARIS FLEA MARKET.

ABOVE: THE BED WAS CUSTOM-MADE IN A TRADITIONAL COLONIAL STYLE AND IS FLANKED BY NINETEENTH-CENTURY CHINESE ARTISTS' CABINETS. THE VINTAGE MOROCCAN RUG WAS FOUND AT NATHAN TURNER IN L.A. **OPPOSITE, TOP LEFT:** FAUX IVORY TUSKS ADD AN AIR OF SAFARI TO THE MASTER BATHROOM. **TOP RIGHT:** EBONIZED TWIN BEDS WITH VOILE MOSQUITO NETTING CONTINUE THE VIBE IN ROCK'S SON'S ROOM. **BOTTOM:** DEBORAH ANDERSON PHOTOGRAPHS ADD SEX APPEAL TO ROCK'S BATHROOM COUNTERTOPS. ANTIQUE IVORY ACCESSORIES FROM GUINEVERE IN LONDON COMPLETE THE LOOK.

Prince of Darkness

ROCK ROYALTY: THE OSBOURNES AT HOME IN HIDDEN HILLS

Every time he sees me, Ozzie Osbourne says "ka ching!" and laughs, as he swears that Sharon, or Mrs. O as I affectionately call her, spends all his money with me. I was introduced to the Osbournes by Elton John, but our friendship really blossomed when Sharon joined the safari in South Africa that Elton arranged for us as a Christmas gift four years ago. Upon returning Sharon asked me to look at the new house she and Ozzie had bought in an exclusive gated community just outside of L.A. After the mad years of their reality show based in their Beverly Hills home, they decided to live a quieter life in this magnificently scaled New England–style home with lots of acreage and sweeping views.

Sharon's days of heavy Gothic-style decorating are over, and now she favors a more French country look, with touches of an English country house thrown in. The couple has some important works of art and an impressive photography collection, as well as some very good antiques, all of which we would use in the new scheme. After several meetings I set to making over the house into a chic environment where the family can relax, their numerous dogs can play, Ozzie can paint (his favorite pastime when not down in his state-of-the-art recording studio in the basement), and Sharon can work in comfort from her beautiful blue and silver wallpapered office, where she supervises the careers of her husband and children, as well as her own unstoppable TV presence.

OPPOSITE: AN EIGHTEENTH-CENTURY FRENCH FIREPLACE ANCHORS THE DINING ROOM AND PLAYS BACKDROP TO AN EARLY LARTIGUE PHOTOGRAPH AND A COLLECTION OF CRYSTAL CROSS-TOPPED VINTAGE BOTTLES. PREVIOUS PAGES, LEFT: UNBELIEVABLY, THIS ANTIQUED MIRROR AND LILAC SILK-LINED BED IS WHERE OZZIE OSBOURNE, THE PRINCE OF DARKNESS, SLEEPS. SILK PAINTED DE GOURNEY "WEEPING WILLOW" WALLPAPER LINES THE WALLS, WHILE SWEDISH-STYLE PAINTED FLOORS ARE EASY FOR LIVING WITH DOGS. RIGHT: A BEDROOM WINDOW FRAMES THE SWEEPING HILLS OF MALIBU.

The living room is decorated around a pair of monumental pale-blue painted Victorian barn doors that slide open to reveal a dream country kitchen. The dining room is very modern-rock-star, with chinoiserie-painted scenes on silver-leafed panels that clad the walls. An amethyst and rock crystal nineteenth-century chandelier from John J. Nelson Antiques sparkles in the central space. I made a faux-ivory-banded ebonized Louis Philippe–style dining table to complement the silver-leafed Louis XVI dining chairs. Glass decanters topped with crystal crosses are scattered with abandon upon all surfaces.

The dreamy master bedroom is a vision of lilac silk and pale grisaille satin, with hand-painted wallpaper panels from de Gournay depicting weeping willow branches. The centerpiece is a magnificent completely mirrored four-poster bed inspired by design icon Bunny Williams's own bedroom. The fact that this is where the Prince of Darkness sleeps is surprising to say the least. (It does, however, have one redeeming macho feature: at the touch of a button a television appears from beneath the bed and swivels into whatever position you desire.)

The Osbourne residence is a beautiful and unexpected home for rock star royalty and was truly one of the most fun projects I have ever undertaken. When I was named Andrew Martin International Interior Designer of the Year in 2010, Sharon and Kelly presented the award, which made the honor all the more special.

IN SHARON'S PRIVATE SITTING ROOM ADJOINING THE MASTER BEDROOM, A CUSTOM SILK VELVET SOFA OFFERS HER A SPOT TO READ WHILE SURROUNDED BY HER BELOVED COLLECTION OF PRE-RAPHAELITE PAINTINGS. AN EIGHTEENTH-CENTURY SILVER-LEAFED ROCOCO-STYLE PEDIMENT FRAMES THE DOORWAY.

ABOVE: A CORNER SOFA IN SHARON'S OFFICE IS UPHOLSTERED IN WHITE COTTON VELVET. THE WALLS, WITH WALLPAPER FROM FARROW AND BALL, ARE HUNG WITH VINTAGE PHOTOGRAPHS OF COCO CHANEL AND HER FASHIONS. **LEFT:** A DETAIL OF SHARON'S MIRRORED JANSEN DESK WITH PICTURES OF HER HUSBAND AND CHILDREN. **OPPOSITE:** PAINTED VICTORIAN BARN DOORS SLIDE OPEN TO REVEAL THE KITCHEN. A CUSTOM SOFA IS SLIPCOVERED IN BLUE LINEN AND DRESSED WITH PETER DUNHAM PILLOWS. THE FAUX IVORY MAHARAJAH COFFEE TABLE IS FROM MY OWN COLLECTION. NINETEENTH-CENTURY FRENCH GRISAILLE BALLROOM CHAIRS PROVIDE EXTRA SEATING. **PREVIOUS PAGES, LEFT:** AN EIGHTEENTH-CENTURY SWEDISH CONSOLE IS SET AGAINST SILVER FOIL–PAINTED DE GOURNEY CHINOISERIE WALLPAPER. A FINE RENOIR PAINTING IS FRAMED IN SILVER-LEAF. **RIGHT:** THE LOUIS PHILIPPE EBONIZED DINING TABLE HAS FAUX *IVOIRE* PAINTED DETAIL ON TOP. A SILVER LEAF CEILING ENHANCES THE ETHEREAL FEEL OF THE ROOM, AND THE TURQUOISE EDELMAN LEATHER OF THE CHAIRS MATCHES THE SCHUMACHER SILK DRAPERIES. THE FRENCH ROCK CRYSTAL AND AMETHYST CHANDELIER IS FROM JOHN NELSON ANTIQUES.

House Call

ELLEN POMPEO'S HISTORIC HOLLYWOOD VILLA

I met met Ellen Pompeo and Chris Ivery unexpectedly in the front row of a winter Christian Dior by John Galliano fashion show in the Tuileries garden of Paris. I was there to accompany Cher, who was running incredibly late that day, so I went ahead to save the seats. Cher eventually arrived during the first runway strut and was seated by the exit while I enjoyed the spectacular front row with Ellen and Chris. Cut to a rainy Sunday two months later, and while shopping in Barneys on Wilshire Boulevard I suddenly heard, "Hello Martyn. How's the front row treating you?" It was Ellen and Chris. We struck up conversation, thrilled to see each other, and promised to get together soon. Upon numerous exchanges I realized we were neighbors—literally five minutes' walk from each other. I insisted they attend a dinner for my wonderful actor friends Ioan Gruffudd and Alice Evans, and by the end of dinner Ellen asked me to help them pull together their very special Whitley Heights house. The result is a fresh, modern interpretation on classic Mediterranean decor.

Ellen, Chris, and daughter Stella Luna are a laid-back, loving family. It was vitally important to give them complete comfort and freedom in their decor. You can sit wherever you like and feel completely at home. The architecture has been allowed to star in this interior, but the rooms flow with comfort and ease. Ellen's love of *Côte Sud* is evident in every room, especially the kitchen, where she has perfected the art of simple, healthy, mouthwatering French and Italian country cuisine. It's my favorite spot to spend Sunday brunch, with delicious food, crisp Italian white wine, dreamy architecture, and a very special young family.

OPPOSITE: ELLEN LOUNGES ON A CUSTOM-MADE EBONIZED MOROCCAN-STYLE SOFA SURROUNDED BY PILLOWS MADE OF TURKISH AND AFGHAN FABRICS. **PREVIOUS PAGES:** A POLYCHROMED TEAK SOFA OF INDIAN INFLUENCE WAS DESIGNED TO BRING AN EXOTIC TOUCH TO ELLEN'S OTHERWISE CLASSICALLY ITALIAN-STYLE GARDEN AND POOL. STRIPED PILLOWS ARE MADE OF PERENNIALS OUTDOOR FABRIC.

"*This house is perfect for our family. It's all about swimming, eating, and hanging out with friends.* — ELLEN POMPEO"

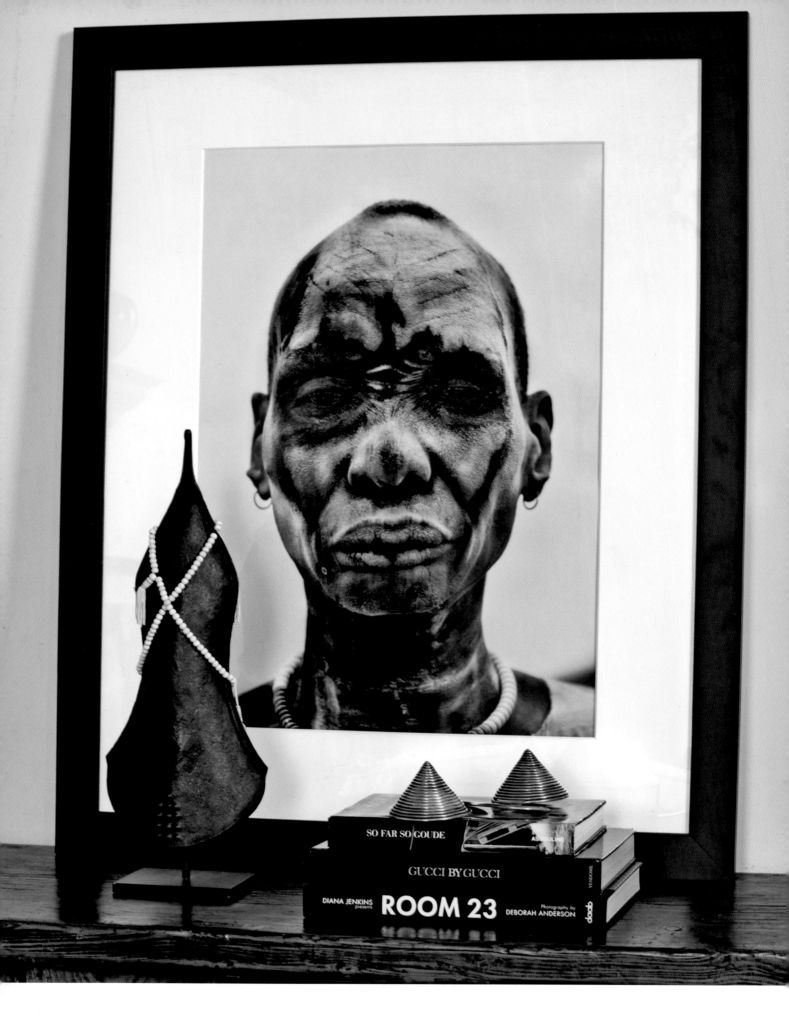

ABOVE: LEANING ON A TABLE IN THE LIVING ROOM IS A POWERFUL PHOTOGRAPHIC PORTRAIT OF AN AFRICAN WARRIOR SURROUNDED BY ANTIQUE AFRICAN "CURRENCY" PIECES. **OPPOSITE:** THE LIVING ROOM CEILING SOARS TO EIGHTEEN FEET, WITH IMPRESSIVE METAL-FRAMED WINDOWS ALLOWING SUNLIGHT TO STREAM IN. A VINTAGE AFGHAN RUG FROM AMADI CARPETS FILLS THE FLOOR, WHILE MOROCCAN TEA TABLES FROM CARAVANE CHAMBRE 19 IN PARIS MIX WELL WITH A 1950S OSVALDO BORSANI LACQUERED VELLUM-TOPPED SIDE TABLE.

THE SIMPLICITY OF THE DINING
ROOM EVOKES ELLEN'S STYLE
PERFECTLY. THE PIERCED
NICKEL LANTERNS THROW
BEAUTIFUL SHADOWS ON THE
WALLS AT NIGHT, WHILE THE
BUGATTI-INSPIRED MIRROR,
ORIGINALLY DESIGNED FOR
CHER AND NOW PART OF MY
FURNITURE COLLECTION, ADDS
AN ELEMENT OF THE EXOTIC.
THE BRASS CANDLESTICK IS
EIGHTEENTH-CENTURY TURKISH.

TOP LEFT: I EBONIZED A VICTORIAN OAK TABLE THAT HAD BEEN INHERITED FROM THE ORIGINAL HOMEOWNERS. A MOROCCAN MIRROR AND TRIBAL STOOL SET THE TONE IN THE ENTRY. THE LARGE CHINESE CERAMIC LAMP WAS ONCE A WINE JAR. THE METAL SCULPTURES ARE MADE WITH ANTIQUE AFRICAN TRADING CURRENCY. TOP RIGHT: A FIFTEEN-FOOT MASHRABIYA SCREEN WAS CUSTOM-MADE TO ECHO THE SCALE OF THE WINDOWS. A PAIR OF 1920S BERGERE ARMCHAIRS WERE RESTORED AND UPHOLSTERED IN A NUBBY LINEN TO ADD OLD-WORLD CHARM, AND THE SIDE TABLE IS PREHISTORIC PETRIFIED WOOD. LEFT: FOUR FATIMA MIRRORS FROM MY COLLECTION REPEAT THE MOORISH ELEMENTS, AND A CERAMIC CANDELABRA BY PICASSO ADDS 1950S GLAMOUR TO THE SPACE. OPPOSITE: THIS VIEW OF THE STAIRCASE FROM THE LIVING ROOM IS ENCHANTING IN ITS SIMPLICITY. A PAIR OF FRENCH 1950S RUSH CHAIRS ADDS TO THIS SIMPLE STYLE, AND A NINETEENTH-CENTURY CHINESE PAINTER'S TABLE PROVIDES SOME WEIGHT TO THE SPACE WHILE GIVING THE TWO SEBASTIÃO SALGADO PHOTOGRAPHS A PERFECT PERCH.

THE KITCHEN WAS DESIGNED
TO FEEL VERY EASYGOING
AND INDUSTRIAL, WHILE
THE RECLAIMED ANTIQUE
FRENCH TERRA-COTTA FLOOR
ADDS THAT FEELING OF AGE
TO MATCH THE REST OF
THE HOUSE. THE PIÈCE DE
RÉSISTANCE IN THE KITCHEN,
HOWEVER, IS THE AMAZING
INDIAN TRAIN STATION
PHOTOGRAPH BY BRAZILIAN
MASTER SEBASTIÃO
SALGADO. THIS PHOTOGRAPH
REPORTEDLY INSPIRED THE
FINAL SCENE IN THE MOVIE
SLUMDOG MILLIONAIRE. THE
INDIAN COTTON DHURRIE
BALANCES THE STRENGTH OF
THE PHOTOGRAPH.

ABOVE: A CURTAINED ARBOR OFF THE MEDIA ROOM CREATES AN INTIMATE SETTING FOR ELLEN TO SERVE A CASUAL DINNER OR JUST READ A SCRIPT. **BELOW:** THE ITALIANATE ARCHITECTURE IS SOFTENED BY VINTAGE STONE URNS. **RIGHT:** THE MASTER BED IS CROWNED WITH AN EGYPTIAN TEXTILE FROM THE 1920S. GRAY LACQUER EDWARD WORMLEY CHESTS SERVE AS NIGHT STANDS, TOPPED WITH 1950S PIERCED-BRASS LANTERNS FOUND IN THE VINTAGE STORE ORANGE IN L.A. A GRAY CALVIN KLEIN CASHMERE BLANKET COVERS THE BED, ACCESSORIZED WITH VINTAGE MOROCCAN AND AFRICAN PILLOWS AND TEXTILES FROM PAT MCGANN.

Dashing Design

A MUSIC MOGUL'S MOROCCAN FANTASY
IN BEVERLY HILLS

I want to feel like I'm on an exotic vacation every day" was the directive that rap mogul and Rocawear creator Damon Dash gave me from his crackling cell phone as he boarded his jet the day after purchasing his new L.A. pad.

Dash, an extraordinary entrepreneur who co-founded Roc-A-Fella Records with Jay Z and discovered talents like Kanye West, wanted his dazzling getaway set high up in Beverly Hills to be a playhouse where he and his family could relax and entertain his L.A. music buddies. It had to be fun, daring, impressive, and sexy. During one of my first design meetings at the house I discovered Macy Gray wandering around the soon-to-be screening room, singing her heart out with earphones and an iPod, completely oblivious to me and my team of curtain makers who were busy measuring around the chanteuse for blackout drapery. (Just one of the many mad encounters I had with urban music legends while doing this project.)

To fulfill this exotic directive we went all-out Moroccan. First we plastered the walls with *tadelakt*, a traditional Moroccan finish. Then I hired Kelly Holden to faux paint the columns to resemble ancient tiles and add intricate baseboard details in the ground-floor public areas, with a triumphant allover stencil in the dining room. The effect from the entry hall is like looking down an enfilade of Moorish paint effects that gain in density the further the eye roams. I used every Moorish trick I knew: tented ceilings, striped walls, pierced fretwork lanterns as electrical fixtures, highly polychromed antique doors from Tangier hung as art, aged mirrors, *Mashrabiya* screens, and tribal-inspired fabrics.

The finished house transports you to a Moroccan riad complete with a harem-style bed in the master bedroom. All that's missing according to Damon's ex-wife, fashion designer Rachel Roy, is a date palm garden to complete their Los Angelina oasis.

OPPOSITE: A TERRACE OVERLOOKING BEL AIR HAS A CUSTOM-MADE MOORISH-STYLE DIVAN FOR LOUNGING IN THE LATE AFTERNOON SUN. **PREVIOUS PAGES, LEFT:** A DETAIL OF THE PAINTED COLUMNS LEADING TO THE LIVING ROOM. **RIGHT:** AN ANTIQUE MOROCCAN DOOR SERVES AS ART ON A LIVING ROOM WALL. NINETEENTH-CENTURY VENETIAN LANTERNS WERE CONVERTED TO STANDING LAMPS, AND AN EIGHTEENTH-CENTURY DUTCH OYSTER-VENEER SIDE TABLE MIXES UP THE LOOK.

THE LIVING ROOM PALETTE
WAS CHOSEN TO ENHANCE
A ROBERT KIME FABRIC THAT
I USED TO UPHOLSTER THE
TURKISH-STYLE SOFAS.
THE BORDER FROM THE
FABRIC WAS CUT AND ADDED
TO THE BASE OF THE SOFAS
AS A TRIM AND ALSO TO
THE LEADING EDGES OF
THE DRAPERY. A VINTAGE
PAINTED TABLE FROM FEZ
HAS MELLOWED WITH AGE
AND ADDS ATMOSPHERE
TO THE ROOM.

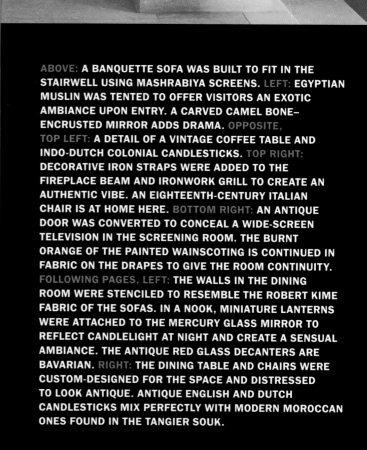

ABOVE: A BANQUETTE SOFA WAS BUILT TO FIT IN THE STAIRWELL USING MASHRABIYA SCREENS. LEFT: EGYPTIAN MUSLIN WAS TENTED TO OFFER VISITORS AN EXOTIC AMBIANCE UPON ENTRY. A CARVED CAMEL BONE–ENCRUSTED MIRROR ADDS DRAMA. OPPOSITE, TOP LEFT: A DETAIL OF A VINTAGE COFFEE TABLE AND INDO-DUTCH COLONIAL CANDLESTICKS. TOP RIGHT: DECORATIVE IRON STRAPS WERE ADDED TO THE FIREPLACE BEAM AND IRONWORK GRILL TO CREATE AN AUTHENTIC VIBE. AN EIGHTEENTH-CENTURY ITALIAN CHAIR IS AT HOME HERE. BOTTOM RIGHT: AN ANTIQUE DOOR WAS CONVERTED TO CONCEAL A WIDE-SCREEN TELEVISION IN THE SCREENING ROOM. THE BURNT ORANGE OF THE PAINTED WAINSCOTING IS CONTINUED IN FABRIC ON THE DRAPES TO GIVE THE ROOM CONTINUITY. FOLLOWING PAGES, LEFT: THE WALLS IN THE DINING ROOM WERE STENCILED TO RESEMBLE THE ROBERT KIME FABRIC OF THE SOFAS. IN A NOOK, MINIATURE LANTERNS WERE ATTACHED TO THE MERCURY GLASS MIRROR TO REFLECT CANDLELIGHT AT NIGHT AND CREATE A SENSUAL AMBIANCE. THE ANTIQUE RED GLASS DECANTERS ARE BAVARIAN. RIGHT: THE DINING TABLE AND CHAIRS WERE CUSTOM-DESIGNED FOR THE SPACE AND DISTRESSED TO LOOK ANTIQUE. ANTIQUE ENGLISH AND DUTCH CANDLESTICKS MIX PERFECTLY WITH MODERN MOROCCAN ONES FOUND IN THE TANGIER SOUK.

ABOVE: **THE MASTER BEDROOM WALLS WERE** *TADELAKT* **PLASTERED BY STEVE LECLAIRE. ANTIQUE MOROCCAN LACE WAS USED FOR THE BED SKIRT.** OPPOSITE, TOP LEFT: **THE DETAILED PAINTWORK THROUGHOUT THE HOUSE TOOK KELLY HOLDEN ONE MONTH TO COMPLETE.** TOP RIGHT AND BOTTOM RIGHT: **THE** *TADELAKT* **PLASTER IN THE HALLS AND POWDER ROOM WAS POLISHED BY HAND.** BOTTOM LEFT: **THE BED, DRESSED IN ANTIQUE SUZANIS I BOUGHT IN ISMIR, WAS CUSTOM MADE TO RESEMBLE ONE I SAW IN A RIAD IN MARRAKESH.**

Regency Redux

HOLLYWOOD REGENCY REINTERPRETED
IN BEVERLY HILLS

I had decorated a large home for writer Aaron Sorkin and his wife, Julia, up in the Hollywood Hills. Julia and I shopped together in London and Paris, finding some exceptional Regency and Georgian furniture, along with Edwardian leather club chairs and myriad accessories. We decorated the home in the English country house manner with a continental collector's eye as inspiration. However, the couple eventually separated and I was asked to decorate both Aaron's chic modern bachelor pad on a fashionable street high above the Sunset Strip and Julia's glamorous Beverly Hills Hollywood Regency home that she bought to share with their daughter, Roxy.

We decided to follow the architectural style of the house and decorate it with a Hollywood Regency flavor, made de rigueur by Billy Haines and Dorothy Draper in the 1940s. The strong black and white checkerboard marble floor sets the tone in the entry, flanked by a chinoiserie-influenced dining room on one side and a full-on glamorous living room on the other—all linked together by bursts of turquoise.

The home is designed for comfortable entertaining of every kind (Julia, an extraordinary philanthropist, often opens her home for fundraisers to support PS Arts and other such worthy causes), with its cozy bar room, large flowing kitchen and family room, and outdoor fireplace and cooking stations. Deep sofas and chaises abound, and beautiful, casual guest rooms invite friends to stay. The basement was converted into a theater where Roxy and her friends perform plays written by her Oscar-winning father. With its fanciful color palette, the home feels young and fresh, while still retaining its classical roots.

OPPOSITE: STARK CHINESE SILK PAINTED WALLPAPER IS THE PERFECT BACKDROP FOR THE DINING ROOM. PREVIOUS PAGES: THE GRAPHIC BLACK AND WHITE MARBLE FLOOR SETS THE TONE FOR THE HOME IN THE ENTRY. THE CONSOLES ARE POILLERAT. BOTH THE MARBLE TAZZA AND THE FEMALE TORSO WERE FOUND ON A BUYING TRIP WITH JULIA TO LONDON AT THE GROSVENOR HOUSE ART & ANTIQUES FAIR. THE CHAIR IS FROM BILLY HAINES DESIGNS. FOLLOWING PAGES: THE LIVING ROOM SOFA WAS COVERED IN TURQUOISE SILK VELVET FROM LARSEN. THE SILVER-LEAF SCREEN WAS CUSTOM-DESIGNED FOR THE SPACE. THE PINK SATIN-COVERED CHAIRS ARE FROM JEAN DE MERRY.

ABOVE: THE REGENCY-STYLE MANTEL
MIRROR WAS DESIGNED TO FIT THE SPACE.
THE ZEBRA OTTOMAN OPENS FOR STORAGE
OF FAMILY PHOTO ALBUMS. LEFT: JULIA AND
AARON SORKIN'S DAUGHTER, ROXY, PUTS ON
A PLAY WITH HER FRIEND IN THE THEATER.
OPPOSITE: THE COZY BAR WAS PAINTED IN
BENJAMIN MOORE CHOCOLATE. THE VINTAGE
ZEBRA RUG ONCE BELONGED TO FAMED
HOLLYWOOD DECORATOR KALEF ALATON,
AND THE CLASSIC FRITZ HENNINGSEN
CHAIR GIVES THE ROOM A TOUCH OF 1950S
GLAMOUR. FOLLOWING PAGES: THE DINING
TABLE I DESIGNED WAS INSPIRED FROM
ONE IN THE BRIGHTON PAVILION. THE FAUX
IVORY DETAIL GIVES IT LIFE. THE LOUIS
XVI–STYLE CHAIRS WERE COVERED IN
TURQUOISE INNOVATIONS LEATHER. THE
CEILING IS WHITE-GOLD-LEAFED TO REFLECT
CANDLELIGHT PERFECTLY AT NIGHT.

OPPOSITE: SURROUNDING
THE KITCHEN TABLE ARE
1940S CHAIRS, WHILE
CUSTOM-MADE BAR STOOLS
SIT AT THE STATUARY-
MARBLE-TOPPED ISLAND.
A POT RACK FROM ANN-
MORRIS ANTIQUES DEFINES
THE SPACE. THE BOTANICAL
PRINTS ARE FROM JOHN
DERIAN'S SHOP IN NEW
YORK CITY. **FOLLOWING
PAGES:** IN THE MASTER
BEDROOM MY FAUX IVORY
JAIPUR BED IS DRESSED IN
A SHEER BRONZE-TONED
PAISLEY FROM OSBORNE &
LITTLE. THE SHADED MINK
PILLOWS ARE FROM FRETTE,
AND THE CASHMERE
BLANKET IS FROM HERMÈS.
THE 1930S MURANO GLASS
LAMPS WERE FOUND AT
DOWNTOWN IN L.A.

ABOVE: IN JULIA'S HOME OFFICE, ZEBRA-COVERED CHAIRS FANCIFULLY PLAY AGAINST THE OLD WORLD WEAVERS WALLPAPER. THE VINTAGE TURQUOISE POTTERY GIVES A CHEERFUL BURST OF COLOR. OPPOSITE, TOP: IN THE GARDEN WE BUILT AN OUTDOOR FIREPLACE TO CREATE A FUN SEATING ARRANGEMENT. TRADITIONAL INDOOR SOFA SHAPES WERE COVERED IN AN OUTDOOR PERENNIALS STRIPE, WHILE THE TEAK-FRAMED CHAIRS AND OTTOMAN WERE COVERED IN FAUX LEATHER. THE STAG'S HEAD SCULPTURE, MADE FROM FIBERGLASS AND STAINLESS STEEL, GIVES THE SPACE SOME HUMOR. WHITE LACQUER TRAYS FROM WILLIAMS-SONOMA SIT ATOP THE OTTOMAN FOR DRINKS AND SNACKS. BOTTOM LEFT: THE MASTER BATH WAS COMPLETELY MIRRORED FOR ABSOLUTE 1940S GLAMOUR. BOTTOM RIGHT: A BIEDERMEIER SLEIGH BED WAS LACQUERED WHITE FOR A GUEST BEDROOM. I UPHOLSTERED THE WALLS IN MY TURKISH TICKING, WHICH IS THE PERFECT BACKDROP FOR THE SLIM AARONS PHOTOGRAPH OF C.Z. GUEST. A FRITZ HENNINGSEN WING CHAIR GROUNDS THE SPACE.

If the Shoe Fits

TAMARA MELLON'S LUXURIOUS NEW YORK PENTHOUSE

Tamara Mellon, OBE—founder, designer, and muse of the luxury brand Jimmy Choo—is not only one of the chicest, smartest, and sexiest women I know, she is also an amazing design partner.

I had the pleasure of designing her London home, as well as the new in-house Jimmy Choo stores in the Selfridges in London and Osaka, and this apartment is our new baby. Located on the Upper East Side of New York City, the building is of great historical and architectural interest, having once been an exclusive nineteenth-century school. Tamara's penthouse spans the top two floors, with nine thousand square feet of living space and a further five thousand square feet of terraces—almost unheard of in New York City.

The goal was to create a comfortable home where Tamara can relax, work, entertain, and play with her daughter, Minty. Tamara lives her brand, so her home has to be an extension of that: beautiful, luxurious, and cutting-edge, yet rooted in the smartest of traditions. We decided that this look called for an eclectic mix of 1970s chic, 1940s glamour, exotic twists, a David Hicks color palette, and signature Jimmy Choo prints.

Starting with the golden tea-papered entry, I black-lacquered all the wood moldings for a kind of Halston-disco-chic vibe. We added a Terence Koh neon sculpture and a Marilyn Minter photograph of a Jimmy Choo shoe dripping in a golden liquid.

The living room is pure glamour, designed so Tamara can entertain everyone from members of the fashion world to politicians (she has recently become the

OPPOSITE: SILVERED TEA PAPER LINES THE WALLS OF THE ENTRY, WITH A WHIMSICAL NEON SCULPTURE BY TERENCE KOH. A RED VINTAGE VENINI CHANDELIER PROVIDES A WELCOMING GLOW TO THE SPACE.
PREVIOUS PAGES: TAMARA MELLON LOUNGES ON HER CUSTOM-MADE CHESTERFIELD SOFA BELOW A SERIES OF GUIDO MOCAFICO SNAKE PHOTOGRAPHS.

ABOVE: A MARILYN MINTER PHOTOGRAPH OF A JIMMY CHOO SHOE ANNOUNCES TO GUESTS WHOSE HOME THEY'RE IN. THE BRASS
SKYSCRAPER STOOLS ARE BY PAUL EVANS, AND THE RED LEATHER ON THE SOFA IS FROM HOLLY HUNT. OPPOSITE: THE FIREPLACE
IN THE LIVING ROOM WAS BLACK LACQUERED. THE TERRA-COTTA LINEN WALLS ARE THE PERFECT BACKGROUND TO DISPLAY THE
BRASS CURTIS JERE WALL SCULPTURE, WHILE THE SCAGLIOLA KARL SPRINGER TUSKS ADD A 1970S HALSTON ELEMENT.

ambassador for world trade for the British government). Comfort was not forgotten, however. Every sofa is deep and filled with the softest down, while the floor is covered in a custom-stenciled Jimmy Choo leopard-print rug made of rabbit fur—soft to the touch and glamorous to the eyes.

Tamara and her daughter's favorite room is the library/media room, where Tamara designs her fashion-forward creations during the day, and at night they snuggle in to watch movies and favorite TV shows.

Her haven is her bedroom, with a rare Turkish tapestry of gold thread used as the headboard to her bed, and of course her closet, containing a mere eight hundred pairs of Jimmy Choo shoes and more than two hundred handbags of every style, skin, and color. It is a girl's dream that has certainly come true for this wonderful and talented friend of mine.

OPPOSITE: IN THE DINING AREA, A VINTAGE ALBRIZZI LUCITE DINING TABLE IS SURROUNDED BY JACQUES ADNET CHAIRS. THE 1940S MIRRORED COLUMNS DISPLAY 1960S VENINI VASES. **PREVIOUS PAGES:** THE LIVING ROOM CEILING IS COVERED IN GOLDEN TEA PAPER SQUARES. LYING ATOP THE PARQUET FLOOR IS A CUSTOM-STENCILED RABBIT FUR RUG IN THE JIMMY CHOO LEOPARD PATTERN. THE COFFEE TABLE WAS MADE TO MY DESIGN BY LAWSON-FENNING. THE PHOTOGRAPH IS FROM A *VOGUE* FASHION SHOOT BY JIM DINE IN 1967.

TOP FROM LEFT: A SERGE ROCHE
CONSOLE. TWO DETAILS OF BRONZE
SCULPTURES AROUND THE HOME.
CENTER FROM LEFT: THE BASE OF
THE DESK IN THE MEDIA ROOM. A
BRONZE CLOCK. A DETAIL OF THE
EMBROIDERED GUEST BEDROOM
BED. LEFT: DAVID HICKS WALLPAPER
IN THE POWDER ROOM. RIGHT: A
FORNASETTI VASE HOLDS POPPIES.
OPPOSITE: ASSORTED ITALIAN
ART GLASS VASES DECORATE A
LIVING ROOM CONSOLE. PREVIOUS
PAGES: THE LUXURIOUS MEDIA
ROOM FLOOR IS COVERED IN A RUG
COMPANY ALPACA. THE VINTAGE
DESK IS BY MAISON JANSEN, AND
THE GLASS LAMP IS EARLY 1970S
PIERRE CARDIN.

ABOVE LEFT: A JIM DINE FASHION PHOTOGRAPH SPICES UP THE WALLS IN THE MASTER BEDROOM. LACQUERED JEAN DE MERRY CHAIRS ARE COVERED IN CREAM ALLIGATOR. THE BRONZE SIDE TABLE WAS GILDED. ABOVE: A CUSTOM CLOSET WAS BUILT TO HOUSE TAMARA'S CURRENT SEASON SHOE COLLECTION, TOTALING MORE THAN EIGHT HUNDRED PAIRS OF JIMMY CHOOS AND TWO-HUNDRED-PLUS PURSES OF EVERY POSSIBLE CONFIGURATION.
LEFT: THE BATHROOM HAS A FOOTED WATERWORKS TUB AND GLAMOROUS MIRRORED WALLS. TWO HORST P. HORST PHOTOGRAPHS ARE MOUNTED UPON THE MIRROR. A PAIR OF GIO PONTI STOOLS COVERED IN MONGOLIAN LAMB ADDS A MODERNIST TWIST. THE CHANDELIER IS 1960S FROM VINCENZO CAFFERELLA. OPPOSITE: THE BEDROOM WALLS, COVERED IN ABACADAZZLE BY MAYA ROMANOFF, SPARKLE SLIGHTLY AT NIGHT. THE EIGHTEENTH-CENTURY HEADBOARD IS MADE FROM A FABRIC PANEL FOUND ON A TRIP TO THE GRAND BAZAAR IN ISTANBUL WITH TAMARA SEVERAL YEARS AGO. IT WAS EMBROIDERED WITH PURE GOLD THREAD TO RESEMBLE THE TREE OF LIFE. THE BEDSIDE LAMPS ARE 1970S ITALIAN. THE BRASS SPUTNIK CHANDELIER IS FROM REFORM, AND THE LEATHER BED SKIRT WAS CUSTOM MADE TO ADD A LITTLE ROCK 'N' ROLL EDGE. BY THE SIDE OF THE BED IS A SELF-PORTRAITS PHOTOGRAPH BY ANDY WARHOL.

"I live my brand: it is my life, my creation, and my passion. My home feeds the fires of my creativity." —TAMARA MELLON

OPPOSITE: TAMARA READS A BOOK ON MINTY'S BED. THE BEDDING IS MADE FROM MY LILAC SULTAN'S SUZANI FABRIC. THE HEADBOARD IS AN EARLY TWENTIETH-CENTURY UZBEK TEXTILE, AND THE FOOTBALL IS ARTFULLY DECORATED BY MIRAKAMI.
ABOVE: A TEPEE IS SET UP FOR PLAY IN MINTY'S BEDROOM. MY SUZANI RUG FOR THE RUG COMPANY COVERS THE FLOOR, AND TWO 1920S FRENCH ARMCHAIRS ARE COVERED IN PINK LEATHER. THE LAMPSHADE FABRIC IS BY MANUEL CANOVAS.

ACKNOWLEDGMENTS

To my mother, Rosina Bullard, who has loved me unconditionally and been my number-one fan, and to my three sisters, Maria Gunstone, Sheila Houghton, and Tina Bullard, whose love, support, and friendship have made me the successful man I am today.

Dearest Yvonne, my mum #2. Your encouragement when I wanted to move to L.A. and start a new career has led me to this path. I am so lucky to have you in my life.

Michael Green, you are my rock star. Your patience with me during the writing of this book has been amazing, and your support and love made it happen. Words cannot explain how grateful I am to you.

To my amazing clients over the years, whose trust and passion have allowed me to create beautiful interiors that reflect our bond together, thank you so very much. Cheryl Tiegs: you are the most amazing friend anyone could ever wish for. Sir Elton John, David Furnish, and baby Zachary: words cannot express how much I love you guys. I am so grateful to have you in my life. Cher: what fun we have had over the years. Your passion for decorating is inspirational. Joe Francis, my Aries buddy, I will never forget our Mexican adventures, ever! Dearest Carolyn Dirks, you are my L.A. mum and a great joy in my life. And Brett Dougherty, what an adoring and fun-loving friend you are. Chris Cortazzo, my partner in crime, best mate, and incredible supporter. I have loved every second of our friendship. Kid Rock—Bobby—what a talent you are. And one of the coolest dudes around. Ozzie and Mrs. O, my rock 'n' roll family. For all the love and laughter you have given me, I am eternally grateful. Ellen Pompeo, Chris Ivery, and Stella Luna: you are the ideal family in every way, and I enjoy every minute I spend with you. Damon Dash: now that was one fun ride! Julia Sorkin: not only do we share a birthday, but we are soul mates. I adore you so. Tamara Mellon, one of my oldest friends. I love you so. Your support of my career has been phenomenal, and our collaborations have brought me nothing but joy. Minty, you will have my heart forever.

To my wonderful, loyal friends, who have supported me with your love and incredible PR: Diana Jenkins (you're at the top of this list for sure!) Liz Heller and John Manulis, Evgeny Lebedev, Christine Cox, Sara Ell, Ian Proetta, Deborah Anderson, Loree Rodkin, Kelly Osbourne, Stacey Dash, Nebi Koc, RuPaul Charles, Minnie Driver, Miriam Rothbart, Ulf Andersson, Sisa Mwenge, Melissa Odabash, Fru Throlstrop, Downtown Julie Brown, Julie Dennis, Linda McQueen, and the divine Tamara Beckwith. You are all such important people in my life. You inspire me, you make me laugh, and you know how to have a really good time!

To my incredible office staff, you have all been amazing, and without you I could never have done what I've done. I especially thank Jim Marden, who expertly juggles my office with kid gloves; Matt Stokes, my architect extraordinaire; Boby Ismirnioglou, who somehow balances my American Express bills; Amanda Paul, Elissa Silver, Leura Fine, and Brian Ferrick, you have all worked so hard and I'm so very grateful.

Margaret Russell, you have not only tirelessly published my work in *Elle Décor* and now in *Architectural Digest*, you have become a great friend. Your support has without doubt changed the course of my career. Michael Bodro, Anita Sarsidi, and everyone at *Elle Décor*, I thank you for putting me in your über-chic pages. Newell Turner and dear Doretta Sperduto, thank you for the beautiful layouts you have done for me over the years at *House Beautiful*. Christine Pittel, you are the best writer! Dara Caponigro, what fun we have had. Thank you and everyone at *Veranda* for your support and two spectacular showcase houses. Carolyn Englefield, you are a hoot! Jenny Bradley at *Traditional Home*: you've always been such a pleasure to work with. Thank you so much. Pamela Lerner Jaccarino and Jo Campbell-Fujii, you guys at *Luxe* are the best—always full of laughter and energy. Jennifer Smith Hale and Andrea Stanford, I love being in *C* magazine. Such beautiful quality features and always so much fun to work with you both. Michael Bruno, your creative energy is astounding. The power of 1stdibs is now legendary, and so are you!

Many thanks to all my friends at Schumacher who have made my collection there possible. Susan North and Liz Nightingale, especially—so fun to be part of your family. I thank the Rug Company and especially Amanda Price for allowing me to design rugs with abandon for them. To my friends at Verutek, I'm very proud of our fight for the world's ecology and that "Bullard's Best" is helping in that fight, one household at a time.

A big thank you to all the people in the interior design world who have helped me over the years and all the show rooms that represent my products, including Holly Hunt, Grizzel and Mann, Holland and Sherry, Hollywood at Home, Tissus D'Hélène, Tigger Hall, Webster and Co., Schumacher, Guinevere, and Thomas Lavin.

Carlos Motta, florist extraordinaire, purveyor of all things stylish and hilarious, riotous friend: your talent astounds me.

My ex-business partner, Trip Haenisch, I thank you for teaching me the business of the business. We created some truly beautiful interiors together and had a lot of fun doing it.

To my wonderfully creative and talented interior designer friends, Kathryn Ireland, Windsor Smith, Nathan Turner, Peter Dunham, and Timothy Whealon. I love you all, and your work inspires me daily.

Tim Street-Porter for the amazing photos you have taken of my work over the years. The beauty you have captured is documented now for all to see in this book—a true testament to your outstanding talent.

Dear Annie Kelly, your support of this book and its creation from start to finish is truly appreciated. Thank you for your knowledge and love.

Huge thanks to all the other very talented photographers who have contributed their work and outstanding portraiture to this project: the sexy Douglas Friedman; the iconic Harry Benson; Firooz Zahedi, I love your shot of Ellen Pompeo (you are also the most amazing chef!); John Ellis; François Dischinger; and last, but not least, my dearest friend, the multitalented artist Deborah Anderson.

My wonderful PR team: Karine Joret and all your cute girls at Joret Group. What a wonderful job you have done for me. Much love to you all.

Alexandra Bennaim and your impossibly chic girls, Pauline and Mette. Thank you for creating my worldwide press exposure. You have done the most amazing and thorough job. There cannot possibly be a better PR agency in the whole of Europe than APR!

The great team at Bravo TV, Andy Cohen, and my producers at Goodbye Productions. What fun we had making *Million Dollar Decorators*. Fellow cast members, I could not imagine a more delicious group to tantalize our audience with.

Thank you, David Stanley, for expertly refining my contracts and making everything legal and watertight.

To my super agents at WME, Sean Perry, Amanda Kogan, and Brooke Slavik Jung, I love you guys.

To my UK manager, Vicky White, at White Management, I cannot thank you enough for your belief in me and my career. You're fearless!

Finally, an enormous heartfelt thank you to the huge talents of my team at Rizzoli:

Doug Turshen and David Huang, your spectacular layouts of my book are only surpassed by your wonderful professionalism. My Darling Alexandra Tart, how you made sense of my ramblings I will never know. Thank you so much for the sophisticated edit you did with my writing. What a pleasure to work with you. Sandy Gilbert, I'm eternally grateful for your belief in me. Charles Miers, you have trusted me, allowed me to create the book I wanted, and guided the entire process with panache. Thank you from the bottom of my heart.